D0858528

"Readers wondering whether they have what it takes to become successful entrepreneurs will find a good indication in this informative, entertaining book by the man who founded Avis Rent-A-Car. Numerous examples from the author's career add authority to the text, as Avis concentrates on the appropriate personal and business characteristics for success: a desire to be first, perseverance, the ability to work long hours, willingness to risk all, sufficient start-up money, and a pragmatic approach to business. Useful chapters on working with venture capitalists and bankers are also included, as is material on some of the mistakes Avis has made in his career. A valuable appendix contains a model for evaluating various costs and expenses in a specific company."

—Booklist

"Warren Avis has got a sweet deal for you. It's his new handbook for entrepreneurs, *Take a Chance to Be First.* . . . The founder of Avis Rent-A-Car uses concise prose to blend recommended basic personality traits, management and financial principles into recipes for starting and nurturing new businesses."

—The Wall Street Journal

"This book is easy to read and provides practical advice for the entrepreneur. Avis pays almost as much attention to what's essential for the person playing the entrepreneur's role as he does to what makes the entrepreneurial enterprise work."

—Business Age Bookshelf

Warren Avis

TAKE A CHANCE TO BE FIRST

The Secrets of Entrepreneurial Success

McGRAW-HILL BOOK COMPANY

New York   St. Louis   San Francisco   Auckland   Bogotá
Hamburg   London   Madrid   Milan   Mexico   Montreal   New Delhi
Panama   Paris   São Paulo   Singapore   Sydney   Tokyo   Toronto

Reprinted by arrangement with Macmillan Publishing Company

First McGraw-Hill Paperback edition, 1987

1 2 3 4 5 6 7 8 9 F G R F G R 8 7

ISBN 0-07-002547-9

LIBRARY OF CONGRESS CATALOGING-IN-PUBLICATION DATA

Avis, Warren E.
    Take a chance to be first.
    Includes index.
    1. Success in business.   2. Avis-Rent-A-Car System.
I. Title.
HF5386.A94   1987   650.1   87-13236
ISBN 0-07-002547-9 (pbk.)

Dedicated to all entrepreneurs

Contents

CONTENTS

Acknowledgments

*I*t would be impossible to thank everyone who has contributed to this book, but a few specific words of gratitude are in order.

Many people have shaped my business life and skills over the years, including bankers, lawyers, accountants, business colleagues and other entrepreneurs. But I'm particularly grateful to Sid McNiece, my friend and long-time business associate, for his ongoing advice and support. Many of the experiences that are described in these pages would not have been possible without Sid's help and guidance.

Also, I greatly appreciate the contributions that William Proctor has made in collaborating with me on this book. During the many productive hours we've spent together in head-to-head editorial discussions, I've had an opportunity to crystallize business principles that have guided me implicitly in the past. At the same time, Bill tells me that he has learned a great deal himself—not only about the "nuts and bolts" of my approach to business, but also about the merits of approaching a book-writing assignment as an entrepreneurial project. In particular, he and his editorial associate Kim Flowers are to be commended for their ability to stay with this project through the "follow-through" phase, which I regard as so essential to the successful outcome of any venture.

In addition, I'm indebted to the many friends and colleagues who read the manuscript at various stages and made helpful contributions. Specifically, I'm grateful to Professor Vittorio de Nora for his suggestions and observations.

Finally, I want to thank my wife, Yanna, for her help and patience both in reading and evaluating the manuscript, and also in putting up with my all-consuming involvement at various times in this project.

WARREN AVIS

TAKE A CHANCE TO BE FIRST

One

The Great Entrepreneurial Adventure

"It was often said . . . that long ago one of the Took ancestors must have taken a fairy wife. That was, of course, absurd, but certainly there was still something not entirely hobbit-like about them, and once in a while members of the Took-clan would go and have adventures. They discreetly disappeared, and the family hushed it up; but the fact remained that the Tooks were not as respectable as the Bagginses, though they were undoubtedly richer."

—*J. R. R. Tolkien,*
The Hobbit

When I started out in business, I had five goals I wanted to achieve:

- I wanted to make a lot of money;
- I wanted plenty of excitement;
- I wanted to be my own boss;
- I wanted to be the best at whatever I did; and
- I wanted to make a contribution to society.

From the very beginning, I did every legitimate thing I could think of to achieve these objectives. Or as Plunkett of Tammany Hall said, "I seen my opportunities and I took 'em." In short, I embarked with total abandon on my own personal adventure over the rough but exhilarating terrain of free enterprise.

In later years, money has receded as a motive, and a need to be creative and to provide significant services for others has come to the fore. But the desire for adventure, independence and a first-place finish has always been strong—so strong, in fact, that I've been involved as a major owner in twenty or thirty businesses, including Avis Rent-A-Car.

I've also come to realize that the entrepreneur is a unique kind of American hero, a person whom many would like to emulate, if only they knew how. The freewheeling independent business-man represents a solution to the deep-seated drive for personal freedom. No matter how exciting our lives may appear from the outside to others, they often seem humdrum to us. So we're constantly looking for ways to break out of the mold. We want to escape from the shackles of our daily, repetitive, often boring responsibilities.

In short, we want to have an adventure.

Some people can be satisfied simply by embarking on adventures in their minds. Through movies, books or just plain daydreaming, they become the dashing jetsetter, the swashbuckling soldier of fortune or the glamorous femme fatale. The Bogart-Bacall armchair escape fantasy fortifies them temporarily for yet another encounter with domestic or bureaucratic boredom.

But many people aren't satisfied merely with going on mental adventures. For them the fun may *start* there. But like the Took clan in Tolkien's classic work *The Hobbit*, they've also got to *do* something about it. That's how history moves forward; how legends spring up; how real heroes are made.

Every age has its adventuresome activists who find some special way to express themselves in the real world. They may become Spanish explorers, English pirates, samurai ronin, American frontiersmen, fearless mercenaries, or firebrand evangelists. Or they may join that peculiar band of independent business gunslingers that we know as the entrepreneurs.

Most historians agree that the age of the American entrepreneur really began to flower back in the late eighteenth and early nineteenth centuries. In earlier years, plenty of free economic spirits had operated in the colonies of the New World. But entrepreneurs didn't find truly firm footing to pursue their pie-in-the-sky schemes until the United States was formally constituted, with its laws favoring independent enterprise.

At this point, the stage was set for one of the most exciting mass escapades of all time—the Great Entrepreneurial Adventure. The French observer, Alexis de Tocqueville, in his classic *Democracy in America*, chronicled the first stages of this development after his trip to the States in the 1830s:

"In democracies nothing is greater or more brilliant than commerce; it attracts the attention of the public and fills the imagination of the multitude; all energetic passions are directed towards it. . . . "

Tocqueville went on to explain the free enterprise phenomenon in terms of the intoxicating impact of financial risk: "Those who live in the midst of democratic fluctuations have always before their eyes the image of *chance*; and they end by liking all undertakings in which chance plays a part. They are therefore all led to engage in commerce, not only for the sake of the profit it holds out to them, but for the love of the constant *excitement* occasioned by that pursuit."

It was a time of feverish and highly profitable fun. But like all good things, the heyday of free enterprise wasn't expected to last forever. In fact, about twenty or so years ago, many had already begun to toll the death knell for the American entrepreneur. Some had actually placed the great hero solemnly in the grave. Full honors, taps, the works.

Sure, the entrepreneur had contributed immeasurably to the development of the American system of free enterprise, not to mention the premier position of the United States in the world economy. The nation's citizens had become affluent on a scale never before known in history—mostly because of this brilliant, independent hotshot. He had been through countless financial wars and with a distinctive flair, he had emerged victorious.

But that was water under the bridge. Now, the entrepreneur's time had passed. He was an anachronism. In fact, he had been pronounced dead. Dead as a doornail.

Or so it was supposed.

Despite the pessimism of many pundits in the 1950s and 1960s, I wasn't convinced. I continued to believe that the entrepreneur was still alive. After all, I *was* one!

But it wasn't easy. I still recall vividly some heated debates I had in those days about the future prospects for the small business operator. One of my chief antagonists was a good friend, one of the world's leading psychologists.

"Real research has moved up to the big companies," he argued. "They have the big staffs and the best research-and-development teams. The little guy has been crushed out."

In some ways, it was a compelling argument. Twenty or thirty years ago, there did seem to be fewer feisty fellows who were able to start up a business in a garage and then build it into a multimillion-dollar enterprise. Also, pundits like John Kenneth Galbraith, in his 1967 bestseller *The New Industrial State*, saw the entrepreneur being replaced as the prime leader in business by the sprawling management of monstrous corporations.

No doubt there was truth in some of these observations. Yet I sensed somehow that I wasn't doomed to be the last of a dying breed. Something told me that the entrepreneur would rise again, in full force. I didn't know how or when it would happen. But I was absolutely sure that it *would* happen. And it did.

Like a phoenix rising youthful and fresh from its own ashes, the American entrepreneur has burst forth on the scene in the last few years with a new vigor that has generated excitement and emulation throughout the world. With high-tech and computer industries leading the way, tiny, one-horse enterprises have taken off overnight.

The news media have chronicled this incredible resurrection, which has ushered in a new entrepreneurial era. To get a flavor of what's been happening, listen to a sampling of what headlines have heralded during the past three years. These reports come from such diverse sources as *The New York Times*, *Reader's Digest*, *The Wall Street Journal*, *The Christian Science Monitor*, *BusinessWeek*, *Forbes*, *Fortune*, you name it:

"A Pioneer Spirit Sweeps Business: Spurred by technology and venture capital, entrepreneurs have made markets and millions"

"America's Dynamic Entrepreneurs: . . . risk-takers are . . . providing two-thirds of all new jobs"

"Today's Sweden Looks to the Entrepreneurs"

"Entrepreneurs in China Are Quick to Seize Opportunity, Despite Official Delays, Hostility"

"Start-up Ventures Blossom in Japan"

The list could go on and on. Clearly, we're speeding along on the crest of an entrepreneurial wave. The American Entrepreneur is riding again at full tilt, and he's issuing a personal challenge to each one of us. If you have an extra dose of courage and a nagging need to break out of the boring routine of life, he's calling you to mount some exciting money-making idea that's been on your mind and bound off on an adventure with him!

Down deep, *practically everyone wants to be an entrepreneur*. In fact, I've never met a wage-earner who doesn't long to own his own business, to work for himself rather than for someone else. Man or woman, young or old—everyone fantasizes about that kind of independence.

Of course, there are a wide variety of factors that may drive people to strike out on their own: Heading the list are a desire to increase personal power, to escape poverty, to build a personal fortune and to be independent. Then, there's the challenge of "another mountain to climb"; a lack of social acceptance; a sense of inferiority; a need to be creative; a commitment to help others; a resolve that "my kids are going to have it better than I did."

In short, the motives are as different as the individuals. But underlying them all is a deep need to control at least some important part of your life. If you're like most people, you want to carve out your own piece of turf and then become a leader—and maybe even *number one*—in this personal fiefdom that you've forged by your own intelligence and efforts.

Of course, it's a big leap from merely wanting success as an entrepreneur to actually achieving it. That's why in the following pages I've attempted to illustrate through my own successes and mistakes, the practical implications of the entrepreneurial personality.

Specifically, it's important to understand:

- Some key personal qualities that may be present in a successful entrepreneur;
- What it really means to be a leader in your chosen field;
- The basic secret to launching a successful business;
- The profits and pitfalls of joining forces with partners;
- How to cross the "Megabucks Border" into big-time business;
- Why loners make lousy entrepreneurs;
- How to avoid the legal entanglements of entrepreneurship;
- Some lessons from the Avis Rent-A-Car experience;
- The implications of mistakes I've made (almost every cloud has a silver lining if you just know where to look for it!); and
- The key axioms for entrepreneurs.

Now, let's begin our exploration of the gunslinging entrepreneurial personality on a personal note—my own experience in founding the Avis Airlines Rent-A-Car Company.

Two

The Avis
Rent-A-Car Adventure

*"A man travels the world over in
search of what he needs and
returns home to find it."*

—George Moore,
The Brook Kerith, *1916*

An entrepreneur may have a series of reasonably significant successes in a variety of different fields during his career. But sometimes, there will be one or two supreme mountaintop achievements. That's what happened when I had the good fortune to formulate the Avis Airlines Rent-A-Car concept while still in my turbulent twenties.

That was a time of high adventure that carried me to an entrepreneurial peak. At the same time, some important principles emerged from the experience that have stuck with me ever since.

The airport car-rental concept first came to me while I was an Air Force combat flying officer during World War II. During that period, I traveled around this country and overseas, including combat zones. No matter where we went, we could never find any decent ground transportation. After we landed, we'd often have to take a taxi to a town that might be fifty miles away. Sometimes, we even carried motorcycles in the bomb bays of our planes so that we'd be able to get around after we landed!

There was absolutely no way at that time to rent an automobile in airports. The Hertz system had moved into many cities around the country—but not into the airports. In 1946 and 1947, business people didn't often rent cars. In fact, rent-a-car offices were frequently located in back-alley garages, with a fleet of old jalopies "at the ready." Credit cards were unknown for this purpose. Also, the process of renting a car on a business trip could be quite laborious. It usually took one to two hours to take an airport taxi into town to the rent-a-car garage and to check out a car. Then, it would involve an hour-long procedure to return the vehicle and go back to the airport by taxi.

Clearly, there was a crying need that had to be satisfied if national and international airline systems were to serve business communities around the world effectively. It sometimes took me longer to get from the airport to the car rental garage and then to my hotel than it did from one airport to another by air!

The idea began to form while I was in the service. I continued to think it through and develop it. Obviously, if a car-rental system was to be set up at airports, it had to be established on a national basis. Passengers traveling to any part of the country had to know that a car would be available for them at any major airport where they might land. Without a national image and network, the concept would lose a lot of its "oomph" and might even fail.

But a major initial problem that I confronted was that there were no national car-rental outlets in any airports at the time. Nobody had tried such a concept. Everyone, including the Hertz people, thought it was impossible. So an extensive public training and education program was going to be necessary to put the idea across and stimulate demand.

To make matters even more difficult, most people I approached for help or advice said that the concept simply wouldn't work. The objections ran the gamut of negative thinking: I was told that a national car-rental system of this type would be impossible to control. There would not be enough demand from business travelers. The cost of buying and maintaining the cars at airports would undermine any profitability. You name it, and the naysayers threw it at me. I suspect that many of these same arguments had convinced Hertz to stay out of the airports.

But I was sure it would work—so sure that I put $10,000 of my own hard-earned capital into the rent-a-car concept to get it started. Also, I borrowed another $75,000, for which I signed personally. That was a sizable sum for a fledgling entrepreneur in the late 1940s. But I had put money aside for just such a purpose. The decision to "invest in myself" was part of my personal philosophy about always putting extra cash to work.

My targets with the car-rental concept were first the Detroit Willow Run airport, and then, Miami. I chose the Detroit airport because I had lived there for many years and knew the area like the back of my hand. Miami was also a natural because it was the hottest car-rental community in the world at that time. People in Florida were always flying in for vacations or business, and growing numbers were getting used to renting cars in the major cities. It was logical that there would also be a lot of possibilities for an airport facility. So we signed exclusive contracts with Willow Run in Detroit and also the Miami airport.

As part of the education process for our consumers, we set up our car-rental counters near the airport baggage pickup area, where people had to wait twenty minutes or so for their luggage. Nobody else wanted this location for business, but it was ideal for us. Many people didn't know how to rent a car in those days; so we took advantage of the baggage delay to explain our system.

Of course, we were confronted with many problems as we tried to work out all the details with the airports. There were endless discussions about exactly where we could place our car-rental counters, the kinds of signs we could put up, and where our parking spaces would be located. At that time, at our insistence, they were always in the parking lot opposite the main terminal.

In addition to the negotiations with the airports, we also had many internal company issues to resolve. These included: the way our rental agreements would be worded; the kind of car insurance we should offer; the kind of people that we wanted to run the rental counters; and the nature of the training that we would give them.

Because we were just getting started in this business, I found myself embroiled in more "hands-on" responsibilities than at practically any other time in my life. I was signing the airport contracts, hiring many of our workers, managing the day-to-day operations, and formulating the strategy that would take us to other major airports in the nation. About all I didn't do was run the rental counters!

At the beginning, we had only about half a dozen people working for us at our airport locations. But soon, we began to grow so quickly that I could see it would be necessary to settle on a fundamental philosophy of how the company was going to be organized.

The issue was clear: (1) I would have to plan on running the details of every one of our rental operations from a central office, and (2) we would have to set up some sort of a licensing arrangement. This latter factor would enable us to secure the best local operators who would take on the responsibility for day-to-day operations in the many cities necessary to make up a national and international company.

I opted for this approach because we didn't have the time, money or ability to run a complete national organization without licensees. We could never grow as fast as we wanted to grow if I had to be entirely responsible overnight for the financing, hiring and management of a nationwide car-rental network.

It was only after having sold Avis Rent-A-Car that I learned about one of my biggest blunders with the licensees. I was quite trusting and rather naive. It didn't dawn on me that some of them might try to cheat by reporting lower revenues than they were actually taking in. Also, I felt I couldn't afford to run auditors all over the country checking up on them. Besides, I didn't want to!

That attitude turned out to be wrong. The people who took over the company from me *did* send out auditors. As a result, they recovered many times more than they had to pay the auditors to investigate. Luckily for me, while I owned the Avis car-rental enterprise, it grew so fast and achieved such incredible success that my mistakes were hardly noticeable.

Our growth exploded like dynamite after we had set up our systems in Detroit and Miami. We worked out a licensing arrangement with a top-notch operator who was already in business in the Miami area. Then we moved into New York, Chicago, Dallas and Washington, D.C., where we set up Avis-owned airport operations.

The basic principles we were following were fairly simple: If we could find good car-rental operators already in place in the cities where we signed up the airports, we would bring them in to run the airport operation. Otherwise we would get everything started and then run it ourselves.

In the early days when business was slow, we could only afford to have one person per counter for each shift during the day. And we couldn't afford to dress them in uniforms. As I was operating on a limited amount of cash, I constantly had to make decisions about where I should invest immediately and where I should wait.

14

An interesting little side issue related to the airport counters that occurred when we were first getting started: I had decided to put young women in charge of the counters, and they were also responsible for taking customers from the counter area to the lots where the cars were parked. That required the women to do a lot of explaining and educating about how the car-rental system worked and then to take customers personally to their cars.

Many people told me, "Girls can't do that sort of thing!" Yet it quickly became evident that women were just as efficient as men in this type of work. Now it's standard procedure to have women in these positions. But at least, with the public's greater familiarity with the system, they don't have to take the customers out to the lots as our women did!

All this attention to detail and careful prior planning quickly began to pay off. Within seven years, Avis had become the world's second largest international rent-a-car system. We had set up hundreds of outlets all over the United States, and we organized Europe on the Avis system years before Hertz even attempted to move in there. We had absolutely no competition from Hertz for the first three years. They remained on the sidelines because they expected that our airport approach wouldn't work, and that I would go broke.

As the business exploded, we found ourselves becoming pioneers in a number of related fields. For example, we originated the rent-a-car credit card concept.

Again, everybody told me that I would lose my shirt with this approach because they expected countless deadbeats to come out of the woodwork. But I knew that the best way we could attract business would be to make it simple for a person to rent a car.

To attract the most creditworthy customers, we convinced the airlines that they should mail out our Avis card with their airline air-travel card. That was a safe and secure move for us. Their card required a $450 deposit, and also, the airlines did credit checks on their customers. So we were able to plug into their preliminary credit screening and thereby save ourselves a great deal of time and money. Also, as part of their mailing, the airlines included a flyer describing how our system worked.

Those were halcyon days for the travel business. We worked hand-in-hand with the airlines and developed our operations together. Our car-rental systems improved the attractiveness of air travel; and of course, the airline growth opened up new business opportunities for us.

But in the midst of this heartfelt good feeling, you might still ask, "What on earth was Hertz doing all this time?"

As I've said, we were the second largest car rental business in the world within seven years, and twenty-five-year-old Hertz, then owned by General Motors, remained number one—but *not* at airports. They strenuously resisted moving into the airports and stuck tenaciously to their downtown rental outlets. Even as we grew by leaps and bounds, the Hertz people vowed up and down that our approach would not work. We began nipping at their heels. But still they waited, sure we would fail.

Then, after about three years, when we had proved that the system *would* work, Hertz made their move. They jumped in and began to copy everything that we had pioneered. I honestly don't think that Hertz has come up with an original idea yet in the airport car-rental field.

During our initial period of growth, hectic though it was, I never had a sense of losing control of our business expansion. One thing that helped me keep a fairly firm handle on our explosive expansion was the fact that we got into the computer field very early.

With the use of the latest high technology, we were able to monitor the work and efficiency of each person assigned to our counters in airports. We could tell how many people should be on a counter at certain times of the day by analyzing the number of rentals that they made and the number of customers they handled.

Of course, when we were building the rent-a-car business in the 1950s, computers were very expensive and cumbersome to use. So even though we installed them at an early date, we also did plenty of analyses of our organization by hand. In many cases, we just pulled out a pencil and paper to determine how many contracts a given person could handle in an hour or in a day. Then, we'd calculate the peaks and valleys in office business.

Using this information, we'd make decisions about whether we were overstaffing or understaffing an office.

Improving our productivity was an issue that was always uppermost in my mind. So as we grew, we constantly looked for patterns that distinguished the efficiency levels of different offices.

We might find one office in one part of the country doing $100,000 a month with ten people on staff. But in another part of the country, we might have fifteen people doing the same $100,000 in business. Obviously, there was some reason to look more closely at that office that had the fifteen people.

In some cases, the management turned out to be incompetent. In other cases, the people on staff needed better training. Sometimes, of course, there might just be an inherent problem in running a rent-a-car counter in a particular airport. If that was the case, we would be confronted with the decision of either living with a less profitable outlet, or perhaps getting the airport management to help us locate a more efficient space.

At other times, a lack of profitability might result from dishonesty. That is, the office with the fifteen people might actually be doing much *more* business than $100,000. But they might have decided to cheat us by reporting a lower income so that the money stayed in their pockets. Whatever the problem, we tried to identify and correct it immediately, so that we could keep our growth and profit on track.

As we continued to grow, it remained obvious that the businessman in those days was the person who really needed our service. But our big problem was to get the word out to him and convince him to buy our service. Because we didn't have a great deal of extra cash to promote and advertise our business, some creativity was in order. So I got in touch with a number of young, aggressive executives in the airline industry, including some hotshot sales managers.

Incidentally, I've learned over the years that it is far more effective to contact people in the middle and upper-middle levels of management, rather than go to the top guy.

I happened to know many of the top guys. And I also knew that popular wisdom said: "Get the chief executive in your pocket, and everybody else will fall into line like dominoes." But don't you believe it!

Without the support of powerful people who are in the middle and upper-middle management ranks, an entrepreneur's proposals are automatically in trouble. The lower-level person with clout can find ways to destroy any project. He can almost always talk a chief executive out of a new project—even one proposed by a friend.

For example, if the boss says, "I like this guy's idea—what do you think?" The sales manager could easily respond, "The quality of service is no good. . . . The price is wrong. . . . These people would never deliver what they say, and they'll give us a black eye in the industry."

So I always checked in with the sales managers and other middle and upper-level executives. And it paid off.

One of the first things that we convinced the airlines to do was to insert Avis pamphlets in the airplane seat pockets. In the past, nothing had ever been allowed in seat pockets other than airline information. But we demonstrated that an Avis airport car would make it possible for a traveler to fly from New York to Chicago or Detroit, transact his business and make it back in one day. Without Avis Airlines Rent-A-Car, it was impossible. So by inserting our thin, low-cost pamphlets in the seats and encouraging our car-rental service, the airlines would also be enhancing their own business.

In many ways, this Avis stuffer was a forerunner of today's in-flight magazines. Although there weren't any magazines on planes in those days, we found that business travelers would read practically everything inserted in those seat pockets, including our extensive explanation of the Avis Rent-A-Car approach. As a result, at very little expense we educated thousands of additional business travelers about how our system worked. As expected, the cooperation of the airlines increased business for both of us.

Then, we took a bold step that almost drove Hertz crazy. I convinced American Airlines to run a cooperative ad with us—one-half page on American, and one-half page on Avis. We each paid for one-half of the advertisement, and I arranged to use American's ad agency to put together our part of the ad. Their agency thus supported us and worked for us, and the cooperative understanding worked like a dream.

These ads were a tremendous help in tying us to the airlines in the public eye. Still, even with the giant steps we were taking to corner the airport car-rental business, we were always short on cash. We had to use the thinnest paper for our various airline-stuffer pamphlets and publications because it cost less money. Also, we first went to the least expensive national business magazine for our full-page cooperative ads with the airlines. In those days, *BusinessWeek* was the one we used. We knew that people usually don't remember the specific magazine where they saw an ad. So if the ad is big and prominent enough in one publication, they tend to think it appeared in *many* magazines. Remember: We were then a fledgling start-up company with little money but a lot of motivation to get a national image.

So even with our limited funds, we succeeded in projecting an image of national stature—mainly because we were associated so closely in the public's mind with American Airlines. Now, the time was ripe, I decided, to try some of the same approaches with the other carriers.

The relationship that we had built up with American set the pace for deals with other airlines. First of all, in our relationship with American, no one had ever asked for a written contract. We were all young, creative, trusting people. There was total mutual trust. It was the same with the other carriers.

In those days, I was so busy I barely wrote letters, much less contracts. I was constantly flying all over America in an effort to set up new offices, negotiate airport contracts, and sign up licensees. Also, I couldn't afford a large home-office staff to take care of the many secretarial and legal matters.

As I contacted the other carriers, I learned that whenever one major airline did something, the others would follow. So in short order, we had the free seat-pocket advertisements and the half-paid, cooperative, full-page magazine ads with most of the other airlines as well.

Finally, with what I realize in retrospect was consummate chutzpah, I went back, first to American and later to the other airlines with my biggest proposal of all: I asked them to give us free teletype service to take Avis reservations.

At first, American Airlines balked a little. They were worried about a number of things, such as what would happen if no cars were available. I solved that one by assuring them that we would give top priority to all their reservations.

Finally, we reached an agreement to test the concept between New York and Detroit. It worked so well—with no complaints—that we moved quickly to establish a free Avis teletype reservation system nationwide with all airlines.

Can you imagine making such a request of one of the airlines today? Believe me, it would be easier to ask one of them for a 747 than to get them to try an innovation like the free Avis teletype system. Today, the airlines handle reservations for such services as car rentals and hotels for a large fee—a development which has been quite profitable for the airlines.

Although we were short of cash in the early stages of this entrepreneurial adventure, we more than made up for it with another rather creative approach to financing—one which actually enabled us to buy our cars at wholesale prices and then sell them later at a higher figure!

Here's how it worked: Before getting into car rentals, I had built up a highly successful Ford dealership in the Detroit area. Clearly, there was a similarity between selling cars and renting them. So I put on my thinking cap and tried to figure out ways that I could tie together the two businesses so as to make them more mutually beneficial.

First, I settled on a strategy that was new for a car-rental company in those days: I decided to buy *new* cars every year for the rent-a-car operation. I wanted our business travelers to get accustomed to a service which provided them with the best possible vehicles and the least possibility of breakdowns. The Ford motor people were very positive about the idea—especially after I pointed out to them that a good car-rental experience would go a long way toward convincing business people to buy a Ford for their own use.

In effect, then, when people rented from us, they would be "test-riding" a Ford. Since General Motors owned Hertz at that time, my argument became even stronger—especially since Hertz, strangely enough, was more in the habit of renting near-jalopies rather than new automobiles.

But perhaps the strongest argument for my decision to link

my two businesses together related to the peculiar state of the postwar economy.

At that time, there was a shortage of cars, and the federal government had set prices for the sale of automobiles to the public. I found if I bought the cars new for the Avis Rent-A-Car business; used them for six months; and then sold them through my Ford dealership, they would be worth more at the time of the sale than they had been when I bought them! In other words, I might buy a car for $1000 (remember, it was 1947!) and then be able to sell it again in the used-car market six months later for $1200—all because cars were in short supply and the federal government was controlling prices!

Most important of all for the Avis reputation, those business people who had never before rented cars were renting our new cars, which rarely had to be serviced. So our customers avoided the hassles and headaches of mechanical breakdowns they had experienced with our competitors. Also, we didn't have to set up an expensive garage system that would have to focus on service and maintenance.

Although this governmental price-control system only lasted for a short time, it provided an important cushion to give us much extra money to grow on. We were able to maintain a very high profit margin in those early years because our cars didn't lose value through depreciation.

As the Avis system grew, the importance of our legal arrangements with the airports quickly became apparent.

We controlled all rent-a-car business in the airports through exclusive contracts. (Although we operated on a handshake with the airlines, everything was in writing with the airports.) So for years Avis was the only car-rental service in major places like Washington National Airport, Miami International Airport, Dallas Love Field and Detroit Metropolitan Airport. These arrangements cleared the way for us to experience maximum growth in Los Angeles, Houston and elsewhere, without worrying about the presence of any competition.

Of course, this situation drove the executives at Hertz even crazier. We simply couldn't see our way to oblige them by going broke; instead, we expanded exponentially!

When we first got started, Hertz president Walter Jacobs

started telling everybody that we were sure to go belly-up, in part because of all the money we were spending on advertising and fast expansion. But as history showed, we didn't go broke; we prospered.

The situation finally got to Jacobs. His people would march into his office, toss our Avis ads on his desk and say, "So this is the guy that's going broke!"

Finally, Jacobs got so mad that he said, "The next son-of-a-bitch that comes in here with a copy of an Avis ad is fired!"

Eventually, Hertz began to move into the airports. But we were years ahead of them. They were always in the position of playing catch-up.

The war with Hertz continued during all the years that I owned the business, but fortunately, our momentum, systems of defense and friendly contacts with the airlines were sufficient to fend them off.

To illustrate the barracuda mentality that prevailed in the rough waters of the early airport car-rental competition, consider a deal that I was trying to work out with a friend who owned another airport rent-a-car company in Florida. This particular company was losing money, and we were thinking of doing a merger with them. But the outfit was so heavily leveraged—so deeply in debt—that we were afraid to take the gamble. It just seemed too risky.

Because we had hesitated at taking that kind of risk, the owner of this company turned elsewhere. He made it a point to talk to me at an airline convention, where we'd be sure to be seen. Then, he mentioned his negotiations with us to the Hertz people—and they didn't think twice about going for the jugular. They immediately offered him an enormous price for his company so that we wouldn't be able to buy it.

The offer was so much more than the company was worth that the man was thrilled to take it; but we remained friendly and loyal to one another. Even after selling and going on the Hertz board of directors, he would speak out during those board meetings, especially when they were making false claims about who started airport car rentals.

That would infuriate the Hertz loyalists. But there was nothing they could do about it because this man had been given the right to sit on their board.

Now, what can we learn from this "car-rental classroom" we've been discussing? There are several lessons that come to mind.

- The big entrepreneurial idea is likely to arise from some big public need. With the Avis system, we saw the need for car rentals at airports, and we rushed in to satisfy it.
- You don't necessarily need a lot of money to found a big operation. But you *do* need highly creative financial concepts to help you stretch your limited resources.
- Excellent business friendships, based on trust, can be an essential ingredient in great entrepreneurial achievement.
- Don't sit on your profits—pump them back into one of your promising enterprises.

I put my Air Force savings into my Ford dealership; and then, in turn, I put my Ford profits into the Avis car-rental system. You work hard—your money should too!

I dreamed up the Avis Airlines Rent-A-Car system when I was an Air Force captain, a flying officer, in my twenties, and sold it while in my thirties for several million. We had reached the point where the business had grown so large that further growth required a full-time manager/caretaker. But as you know, I simply didn't like that role. I was an originator and builder— in short, an entrepreneur.

I feel differently today. I'd like to buy Avis back and make it number one in the world. And I believe this desire is realistic because my ability to run such a business without killing myself has improved.

But the Hertz mentality is still the same as it was when I originally owned Avis. Recently, the current Hertz CEO, Frank Olson, was asked by *The New York Times* (November 10, 1985) what he thought about my desire to take over Avis again—and my intention to turn it into the number one car rental service in the world.

"He can't live that long," Olson said.

My response is that the American public—not the Chief Executive of Hertz—will make that decision, based on the services and prices Avis can provide. The last chapter to this particular story has yet to be written!

In 1954, however, I did what many other entrepreneurs do: I built up the business and then sold out for a handsome profit so that I could move on to other ventures. Also, I wanted to enjoy life—and that didn't include sixteen-hour work days! The difference between my experience and that of many other entrepreneurs is that I was fortunate enough to achieve a fast, phenomenal success. That meant I had plenty of money to play with, plenty to pour into any venture capital project that might catch my fancy.

In short, I was ready at a relatively young age to explore in great depth what it really means to be a "gunslinger" in the American economy.

Three

Are You a Gunslinger?

It was now the Virginian's turn to bet, or leave the game, and he did not speak at once.

Therefore Trampas spoke. "Your bet, you son-of-a———."

The Virginian's pistol came out, and his hand lay on the table, holding it unaimed. And with a voice as gentle as ever, the voice that sounded almost like a caress, but drawling a very little more than usual, so that there was almost a space between each word, he issued his orders to the man Trampas:—

"When you call me that, smile! And he looked at Trampas across the table.

Yes, the voice was gentle. But in my ears, it seemed as if somewhere the bell of death was ringing; and silence like a stroke, fell on the large room.

—Owen Wister,
The Virginian

*T*he dramatic flair and rugged individualism of the old-time gunslinger, frontiersman or explorer have always had the power to pique the imagination. In fact, fantasies of such personal freedom may run wild among modern-day, desk-bound corporate employees who long to escape their humdrum daily schedules.

At one time or another, most workers have felt strongly that they need to shake free of the system; they want to stretch their wings and break away from the constraints of the boring conventions of business-as-usual.

But what kind of personality does it take to strike out on your own—*and* make a success of it?

On one level the answer to this question focuses on the gunslinger myth. In popular thought, the independent, high-rolling business person has often been compared to the swashbuckling adventurer epitomized in the Western tales of Owen Wister or Louis L'Amour. This personality type spans generations and historical epochs. On the American frontier, the term was "gunslinger." On the high seas, it was "pirate." And in Western capitalism, it's "entrepreneur."

Of course, there is some truth to the myth. The best entrepreneurs have some similarities with the old-fashioned adventurers of earlier history. Like the gunslinger, pirate or explorer, the entrepreneur is often unconventional. He's not bound by tradition. He—or she—will tend to come up with a new idea and then run with it in some unexpected, exciting way. He's also willing to put his way of life on the line by taking unusual risks.

At the same time, however, some distinctions have to be made. For one thing, the pirates and gunslingers operated completely outside the law; the entrepreneur, in contrast, must function within the legal system. (Unfortunately, however, our present legal system leaves a lot to be desired. It often permits unethical conduct, if not outright piracy!)

There are some special personal *and* business traits and conditions that distinguish the entrepreneurial personality from all others. These prerequisites—which will be explored both in this chapter and the next—certainly don't represent an exhaustive list. Many entrepreneurs may possess other qualities or benefits which, for them, are equally important. But still, if these conditions are present in your life, you're more likely to strike pay dirt as an entrepreneur. First, we'll consider in some depth the "personal prerequisites" for success; then, we'll turn to the specifically business-related traits.

PERSONAL PREREQUISITE #1:
AN UNENCUMBERED PERSONAL LIFE

Because of the overwhelming obligations and commitments that accompany starting a new venture, many successful entrepreneurs are unmarried. You're just not going to find many successful gunslingers with five or six children and an accumulation of family responsibilities. (In fact, in most home circumstances like this, it would be irresponsible to venture out on your own for the first time—unless you're an extremely unusual and gifted person.)

In those situations where entrepreneurs are married, their spouses often work. In almost every successful case, the spouse is as committed to the venture as the entrepreneur. Otherwise, there's a great danger that the marriage or the venture will fall apart. In short, it is essential that your family, friends and business associates pull you toward and not away from your business goals.

A friend of mine had just outfitted his yacht, and I must say, he had done a beautiful job. But then his wife took one look at what he had done and began to criticize every single thing. As she continued for a while in this vein, I asked, "Don't you realize what you're doing?"

She hadn't the slightest idea. She was destroying her husband without being aware of it. And I knew she had done the same with some of his business ventures. Certainly, he was a success by most standards. But he could have achieved much more and been happier, if only she had built him up instead of tearing him down.

Constant criticizing will often eventually destroy all confidence, whereas a supportive attitude will achieve much more happiness and success. That same principle applies to both men and women, of course. Whether male or female, the victimized spouse always ends up one step farther back in the race to have a successful life, marriage or business.

PERSONAL PREREQUISITE #2:
A SEVERE CASE OF MONOMANIA

The best entrepreneurs have a one-track mind.

One classic new entrepreneur was willing to live in a one-room, cold-water flat by himself. He walked up four flights, spent practically nothing on himself in the way of luxuries and worked eighteen hours a day. In short, he lived and breathed his company. And well he might. This man eventually made it, but only about one in five new ventures succeeds. The others go defunct, regardless of the best intentions and efforts.

So the person who is the inspiration behind a venture must have something extra in the way of personal commitment. It's been said that the successful American business person loves business first, family second, and sports and other things third. There's a lot of truth in that.

In a special report on entrepreneurs published by *The Wall Street Journal* (May 20, 1985), the creator of a successful water-ski company said that he often is preoccupied by business matters, even when he and his family are off somewhere on an outing.

His wife will say, "Talk to me," but instead, he'll pull out a pocket tape recorder and begin dictating some new concept that has come to mind.

"Sometimes, he treats us like workers instead of family," his wife said.

And when asked whether he values family above work, this super-successful entrepreneur replied, "Well, that's a tough one. Of course, you have to say family."

A major corollary to entrepreneurial monomania is the entrepreneur's tendency to take charge of situations outside of work. Entrepreneurs tend to be obsessed with an independent life, and they often chafe under any sort of authority. So whenever there seems to be a vacuum of authority, an entrepreneur will most likely step into it and begin to pull strings, order people around and generally try to take control of the situation.

This can be both a great strength and an obnoxious weakness, as I discovered during one social outing with a friend. We had both been invited to the same social event, and when my friend learned I was staying at the Beverly Hills Hotel, he said, "I'll pick you up, and you can go down with us."

When he pulled up to the hotel, he was sitting in the front seat of a limousine, and the other three of us in the group were in the back. In my typical style, I ordered: "Hey, get out and get in back with us!"

My pal then remarked to the other two, "You see I told you, when Warren arrives, he starts running everything!"

He said it in a nice way, with a nice smile, but it made an enormous impression on me. So I now watch that I don't always tell people what to do. And I've learned that 90 percent of the time if I keep my mouth shut or just make a mild suggestion, what needs to be done gets done anyway.

Certainly, an entrepreneur should try to unwind and enjoy himself when he's not working. But it's not always easy to assume a completely different role when you've been charging ahead with some project, living and breathing it and tossing commands around like some field general.

In fact, during the early stages of a venture, you *have* to be willing to dedicate a good portion of your life to your concept if you hope to make it successful. Otherwise, you're a dilettante; and dilettantes simply aren't competitive in our fast-moving, hard-selling economic environment. It may be true that anybody can create a successful business—but only if there's a willingness to make a near-monomaniacal commitment.

PERSONAL PREREQUISITE #3:
PLENTY OF STAYING POWER

Building a successful business *always* takes longer than the entrepreneur expects. He or she typically believes that the big time will arrive tomorrow. But it's never tomorrow. It's always the day after tomorrow, or the day after that.

I'm that way. Like most entrepreneurs, I always expect to finish a project faster than the time it really takes. I'm firmly convinced it's going to be finished tomorrow. Yet it always takes longer than expected. Even after building a number of successful enterprises, I'm *still* having to learn I have to wait longer; to persevere; to have more patience.

How long can you reasonably expect it will take to turn your business idea into a successful, thriving, profit-producing enterprise?

Typically, it will take between three and five years, from the start of the business to success—though some companies, such as high-tech enterprises, which may turn a huge profit almost immediately, are exceptions to the rule. If you make it big in much less than five years, you're lucky. If you're still struggling after five, maybe you should try another idea or another field—or reassess your management style.

Now, I realize this may seem to be a massive commitment of your life—to put in as much as five years to achieve an entrepreneurial goal. But that's what it takes. You simply have to be in place for a minimum number of years for your idea to build momentum and have a chance to turn a substantial profit. There seems to be some sort of mystical law of the marketplace which requires an input of time, as well as creativity and energy.

This has been a hard lesson for me to learn because I get impatient. I want to see results now—or even better, yesterday. But super-successful gunslinging in any field just isn't like that. Can you imagine Wyatt Earp walking out on a dusty street the first day he ever held a pistol and hitting his target in the center? Of course not! It takes years of practice to perfect the fast draw and the dead-eye aim. And the same principle applies with entrepreneurial gunslinging.

But there's still a temptation in all of us to want to hop over the hard work of preparation and reap all the benefits immediately. Over the years, I've come to realize that my greatest weakness is my unwillingness sometimes to stay with a job as long as necessary to achieve optimum results.

After I have launched a company, I tend to turn to new opportunities. To compensate for this personal trait, I've started to concentrate more on hiring top managers, at attractive salaries and bonuses, to take over when I decide to go on to new ventures. My guess is that I could be worth a hundred times more money if I had just learned to do this years ago. With experienced, competent managers, I can run a company very successfully without being involved in the daily management.

PERSONAL PREREQUISITE #4:
A HIGH ENERGY LEVEL,
NURTURED BY PERIODS OF RELAXATION

Because I'm a very intense person, I need plenty of time off to maintain my staying power year after year. If I didn't pace myself and take good care of my physical and emotional needs, I'd quickly burn out—and I might well run into various health problems.

I began to understand this principle a number of years ago, during one of my first entrepreneurial ventures as an independent sales representative. At the time, I worked for only one company, and the management looked at me as another employee. But there were a number of key differences: For one thing, I worked much harder than the company's average employee. Also, I operated independently—often at unusual hours—and I was paid only by commission.

My inclination to throw myself body and soul into various sales challenges made it necessary for me to pull back periodically to recoup my energies. So from the very beginning, I always gave myself generous vacations.

But when I told a top company executive one year that I planned to take a month off at Christmas, he exploded: "Nobody working with this company ever takes more than two weeks off! And here, you say you're going to take a month!"

"That's right," I said—and I pointed out that unlike many companies we did little business in December anyway.

"Hey, you're *almost* fired!" he said. But he said it with a smile. After all, I was one of his best sales reps. As long as I produced, he really couldn't argue with the month's vacation. But still, he urged me not to mention our little arrangement because it might be bad for company morale, and I agreed.

Unbeknownst to the company, in addition to regular vacations, I also took off plenty of time during the rest of the year as well. So I might put in a sixteen- or eighteen-hour day when going full steam with a project. But then I'd always intersperse my hard work with play and relaxation. Money is no good if you have to work so hard for it you don't have time to enjoy it. If you make twice as much, but don't have time to spend it, what good is it? At least, that was my philosophy. Many people fail to savor life while they're still young, and I certainly didn't want to be like that!

In any case, this company didn't argue with my success. But to live by a "relaxed" philosophy *and* maintain an outstanding sales record, it's necessary to get extremely well organized—and work like hell when the time for work has arrived!

Specifically, my approach was to really work hard for about three weeks each month, and then take the rest of the month off. But during that three weeks, it was necessary to go at top speed, day and night.

I'd get in my car, and drive through Indianapolis, St. Louis, Kansas City and then through other cities in Missouri. The whole itinerary was very precisely laid out; I knew exactly who to see and when to see them. Evenings and lunch hours would be devoted to various clients. It was an extremely packed, intense schedule, but I work best that way.

What's the source of this kind of energy? In part, it helps to be born with it. Many entrepreneurs have enjoyed a healthy level of inner drive and ambition since childhood.

But there's more to it than that. Even after the passing of several decades of entrepreneurial efforts, my energies have waned hardly at all. I attribute this to my ability to have fun and relax, but also to my habits of eating reasonably well and exercising regularly. In some ways, I suppose you might say I'm a health nut.

When on one of my frequent vacations or holidays, I don't just sit around or loll about over snacks or big meals. Rather, my tendency is to stay so busy with either work or leisure activities that I forget about eating.

In fact, I naturally tend to eat only one meal a day—and that's always been the evening meal. But I've learned over the years that I should always plug in one more small snack of fresh fruit each day just to keep my energies up.

Typically, I skip breakfast. But then, I'll make it a point late in the morning to eat some high-fiber, low-cholesterol dish, like All-Bran with skim milk—mainly to provide energy and to reduce the risk of cholesterol or colon cancer. Then, I may have a little fruit around 4 P.M. Finally, when the evening rolls around, I'll usually have fish or some other low-fat dish.

As for exercise, I do a lot of swimming, wind-surfing, jumping horses and water-skiing. The water-skiing may not sound all that strenuous, but it burns up the calories the way I do it: I'll get behind a boat on one ski and sweep back and forth over the wake for as long as an hour. Also, I find some comfort in an old saying that "you won't get arthritis if you water-ski"!

Yet even though I've developed a few personal and health routines, I can't lay out my life in a predictable, exact, evenly spaced way, day after day, month after month, and year after year. I do organize my time effectively; but it's organized according to my special emotional and physical metabolism. I have to go at something very intensely for a short period and then take time off to recoup my energies and interest.

It was quite natural for me to develop this sort of approach at the outset of my career because I was an unfettered bachelor. I had total freedom to go anywhere I wanted and stay with any client or prospect for as long as I felt was warranted.

Of course, it was quite boring on the weekends in many of those towns. That's why I always tried to line up sales meetings on the weekends if I possibly could. I've always hated bars and living alone in a series of boring hotel rooms. But I found I could put up with anything for three weeks at a time. And that was all

I needed to reach the top level of sales with this particular company.

While spending a lot of time in Europe, I've come to realize that the approach to life I developed years ago coincides with what might be called the European view. On the Continent, there's an attitude that making money isn't the ultimate end of all endeavor. Business is just a part of one's existence.

But the typical American loves business. Even when the business person retires—and this is especially true of the executive—he often wants to go back to work. That's because when you're a manager in American business, you have great power over other people; and controlling other people can become a powerful narcotic. Also, if you've never learned to relax and enjoy other things, you get bored.

When the top-level business executive who is an employee, is forced into retirement, he loses a major part of his identity; and that's when the big health problems often begin. Heart attacks often occur soon after retirement, but these people don't just die of a normal heart attack. They die of a broken heart. The phone stops ringing. They're no longer in demand. They failed to make friends apart from their business associates. Also, those goals they had striven for are no longer a possibility for them. And their lives, at least in their view, become worthless.

That's the value of the entrepreneur's way of life. You never have to retire if you're in business for yourself. You can begin to pull back from your responsibilities and time commitments as you get older. But as long as you learn how to develop some staying power, you never have to withdraw completely from the work you love—at least not unless you really want to.

PERSONAL PREREQUISITE #5: GOOD JUDGMENT ABOUT PEOPLE

One of my major problems as an entrepreneur has been my failure to hire the right people to handle enterprises that I begin or buy into. On a number of occasions, it's been too easy to become enchanted by the inspirational sales talk of young business gunslingers, and to trust their thin managerial background—against better business judgment. And more than once, I've lived to regret it.

For example, one obviously intelligent, impressive young hotshot in his mid-twenties had a great idea for a manufacturing project—though it was clear right at the beginning that he needed some "gray hair." In other words, he needed older managers with considerable experience to run the production and financial departments in the company. Unfortunately, he thought he knew it all, and he went broke.

Underlying this is a basic principle of building a successful entrepreneurial venture: You need hard-charging, creative young people (or the classic, Billy-the-Kid-type of gunslinger) *plus* stable, experienced older managers. Without the gray hair, you're often doomed to failure. I wish I had learned this lesson much earlier because I could have avoided many mistakes by including relevant clauses in contracts. All I would have had to do was to require inexperienced partners to hire experienced people where they were needed.

Against my better judgment, another young entrepreneur also talked me into forgetting the experience that goes with the gray hair. So he chose unqualified young friends of his for those experience-related jobs.

Unfortunately, the lack of experience once again quickly began to show. The company almost fell apart with cost overruns and other inefficiencies until experienced people were hired.

I've gotten better at orchestrating the managerial makeup of various companies in recent years—but only after working very hard at improving my lack of good judgment in hiring the right people. With our venture capital operation, it's almost an automatic procedure for us to judge prospective entrepreneurs according to the qualifications of the people they have hired or want to hire. If we don't reach a "meeting of the minds" on this issue, we don't invest.

Specifically, there are five personal features we look for in any prospective business associate: appearance, personality, intelligence, integrity and status.

Appearance. If a person is sloppy, unkempt or otherwise physically unpresentable, he'll immediately have one strike against him. Half of success at any business is getting your foot in the door. And you'll never get your foot in *any* door if you somehow just don't look right.

Two young men approached an investor to get money to finance a venture which was designed to disseminate specialized business information. One of the would-be entrepreneurs was trim and sharply dressed. He *looked* successful. The other, however, was overweight; his top shirt button was open; his tie was askew; and he always seemed to be perspiring and out of breath.

To make a long story short, the investor made a separate appointment with the sharp entrepreneur and suggested, "This is a good idea you have, but why don't you go into this on your own? This other guy is going to hold you back."

In fact, the disheveled young fellow knew more about many of the technical aspects of the venture than his partner. But the investor wouldn't be convinced; and eventually the deal fell through because the sharp entrepreneur insisted on remaining loyal to his untidy cohort.

The moral to this story? Do a devastatingly honest evaluation of your own appearance, and clean up your act before you try to launch any new venture.

Personality. An essential asset for any entrepreneur is a good personality. "Good personality" means the personal quality that makes another person appreciate being around you. People with good personalities tend to be sensitive to the feelings and needs of others, and to be able to communicate their concern effectively. In addition, this involves several "not-beings": *not being* abrasive; *not being* rude; *not being* sarcastic; and *not being* late.

One woman, a boutique owner, has a very sharp wit—and she uses it far too often to poke fun at others, or to make jokes at their expense. She's obviously intelligent and has many other fine qualities. She's also quite attractive—in fact, she spends more than an hour a day making herself look just right. Unfortunately, she doesn't spend even a minute trying to improve her personality by reflecting on her negative effect on other people.

Because she projects a rather unpleasant aura to others, most people prefer not to be around her very long. She's certainly not the first one they think of to do business with or to ask out to social affairs. As a result, she's often unable to attract business contacts who could be a great help as she tries to build her business. In addition, her personal life suffers.

Intelligence. This concept doesn't just refer to IQ or native genius, though certainly, the best entrepreneurs are rather shrewd and bright. Rather, the type of intelligence that really helps a person make a go of a new business is one that involves (1) an ability to communicate, and (2) a capacity to think straight and logically.

In other words, if you have a group of people of only average intelligence and below-average education, they can still put together a thriving enterprise—*if* they can just talk to one another, and to their prospective customers. By communicating effectively, they are in a position to solve their problems more constructively. Also, they'll be better able to work productively together and make effective, joint decisions.

Also, the kind of intelligence that characterizes a successful entrepreneur is one which enables the person to set proper goals and focus on key priorities. One of the major weaknesses among young, inexperienced, would-be entrepreneurs is their inability to narrow their objectives. They tend to be "all over the lot," because they fail to mass their energies and resources to achieve precise objectives.

One very bright young man in the nonprofit field wanted to set up a new religious ministry, but he had many ideas that fascinated him—and he became intent on trying to put all of them into effect. Of course, he lacked the time, ability and financial backing to do everything that interested him. As a result, he accomplished nothing for several years. His career was a total disaster.

Finally, however, he opened his ears to the advice of a couple of friends who had been telling him he needed to focus his considerable skills on one or two things. When he took this approach, he suddenly found his organization growing by leaps and bounds.

So it's not enough just to have a high IQ. You also have to learn practical ways to marshal your brainpower to achieve limited entrepreneurial objectives.

Integrity. You should be able to trust anyone you plan to work with—and they have to be able to trust you. If you tell colleagues or clients you've done something when you haven't, and they find out about it, that's going to erode their trust. Or worse, if you cheat a business associate, you could ruin your reputation in an entrepreneurial field forever. Dishonesty is something that usually throws up an impossible barrier to a working relationship.

One woman was starting off a job search firm which seemed to have tremendous potential, both for herself and for a couple of employees who had gotten in on the ground floor with her.

One Friday, one of the employees, a seemingly bright and promising young man, was given the assignment of mailing a very important package by overnight mail to an important client. But he got involved in some personal business that afternoon and failed to get the package in the mail until the following Monday.

Unfortunately, when he was questioned by his frantic boss that Monday, he lied. He said he had mailed the package as instructed on Friday, and he assumed it must have been lost in the mail. But of course, his lie was uncovered the next day when the package arrived and the client examined the date of mailing which was written clearly on the mailing slip.

This man's employer, the woman who had started the business, seethed for several days about this dishonesty. Finally, she realized she couldn't work with the young man under these circumstances, so she let him go.

The young man ended up missing out on a great opportunity. His other co-worker went on to a responsible and well-paid position as the firm grew. And there's every reason to believe he might have achieved the same level of prestige—if only he had shown some integrity. Unfortunately, most people never realize how much a lack of integrity can cost in the loss of friends and of business success.

Status. This is a tough quality to talk about because when you even raise the issue of status, many people in our egalitarian society think you're trying to be an elitist. But still, I think it's important for an entrepreneur to understand that if he comes across as being of the wrong social status in certain company, he's going to place himself at a decided disadvantage.

What exactly is status?

Having the right status doesn't necessarily mean appearing to be someone who might be in the Social Register. Rather, it just means knowing how to position yourself socially in the group you're trying to influence.

Relatively high status may accompany your education or profession: Doctors, lawyers and others with professional graduate degrees automatically enjoy a high status in most business gatherings. Titles also tend to raise a person's status—president, professor, executive vice president, executive director, chairman, or in Europe inherited titles like duke, count or whatever.

Furthermore, having a significant amount of money—or *appearing* to have money—may add to your status. Also, various achievements, such as honors received, awards earned, or books written, may mean higher status.

Even the town or neighborhood you live in may confer status. In New York, for example, a Park Avenue or Fifth Avenue address will convey more status than one in the outlying sections of Brooklyn or Queens.

None of these things are essential to enable you to fulfill your aspirations to become a successful entrepreneur. But they can certainly help. If your status is perceived as far too low, for example, you may be considered a loser. You'll find yourself always on the outside looking in.

One young entrepreneur had been invited to a party—part-business, part-pleasure—with some high-brow, old-money types. He was looking for supporters for a new venture he had proposed, and he seemed to have everything going for him—sharp looks, a winning personality, obvious intelligence and a reputation for sound integrity. But it quickly became apparent that the young woman he had brought along as a date didn't fit in at all.

During the evening's conversation, she consistently murdered the English language. She made one faux pas after another. Soon, the damage had been done. The young entrepreneur now had a strike against him in the eyes of these investors because his date's social inadequacies had caused his own status to be lowered a notch or two.

It's not necessary to be an elitist—just be realistic! Status is a factor that people use, consciously or subconsciously, in evaluating the business potential of others. And in this particular group, the requirements for status were more stringent than they would be in many other situations. Because this entrepreneur didn't realize this fact, he hurt his chances to get financial backing for his project.

The basic principle here is rather simple: Know the mentality of the people you're dealing with and use common sense. Obviously, bankers don't wear open-neck shirts; so don't wear sloppy or casual clothes to see a banker if you want money from him!

Of course, in some cases, a snooty suggestion of "high status" might hurt. I've run into many situations where it was necessary to project an earthy, good-old-boy image to get potential clients and investors on one's side. In such circumstances, any suggestion of an Ivy League background could hinder rather than enhance your chances.

So when you're thinking of hiring someone, taking on a partner or otherwise evaluating a person, try this five-point evaluation process: Focus on appearance, personality, intelligence, integrity and status. By using this approach, you'll be more likely to exercise sound judgment about people. You might even give yourself the same test periodically, to see how you measure up in the eyes of others. The main idea is to identify your greatest personal weakness, and then try hard to improve it.

These "personal prerequisites" for entrepreneurial success are applicable, of course, to any area of life, including avocations, cultural activities or church work. But they also merge naturally into the second important category, the *business* prerequisites. As we'll see in the next chapter, the most effective gunslinging personality possesses both sets of traits.

Four

The Entrepreneurial Personality

"He has achieved success who has lived well, laughed often and loved much."

—*Bessie Anderson Stanley,*
the prizewinning definition
in a contest sponsored by
Brown Book *magazine, 1904*

*P*ersonal qualities are the bedrock on which any business success must be based. But the ability to operate effectively in specific situations in the real world of commerce and industry is what will ultimately make or break an entrepreneurial venture. To this end, here are some "business prerequisites" which should help polish most individuals into what might be called the entrepreneurial personality."

BUSINESS PREREQUISITE #1: A BELIEF THAT NOTHING IN YOUR BUSINESS IS IMPOSSIBLE

To become great, a person must learn nothing is impossible. But that's not so easy. I've often said that if I had known how many headaches I was going to face in starting the Avis Rent-A-Car company—or for that matter, many of my other ventures—I never would have had the guts to start.

With the rent-a-car company, my problem wasn't money. We were always profitable. But one thing that gave me a great deal of trouble was our rate of expansion. If we grew too fast, we wouldn't be able to put together the management system to run the entire country overnight. Yet at the same time, I had to maintain our momentum and cash flow. That's when I decided to bring in licensees with proven management experience to run new airport outlets in various parts of the country.

Although I knew a few licensees would someday be worth $15 million to $20 million or more if they and we were successful, I made the conscious decision to hand out those licenses *free* to the best operators. That seemed the best way to achieve as quickly as possible our basic mission, which was to build the greatest rent-a-car system in the world.

At the outset, however, I had no inkling of what was involved in selecting and working with licensees. On top of that, I only gradually became aware of all the other headaches with paper-work and the personnel that went along with building an inter-national business.

Quite frankly, if I had known these difficulties ahead of time, I might have been thoroughly discouraged before I even got started. In short, understanding all the pitfalls in a venture can wreck the desire to pursue it. So in a sense, ignorance is bliss for an entre-preneur. Or at least a *degree* of ignorance. Problems that have to be solved *will* be solved, because for the dedicated entrepre-neur, necessity is indeed the "mother of invention."

Finally, if you dwell on the negatives, you will have that much less time for the positives—for the ideas and projects that have a chance to make it. For that reason, an entrepreneur should focus on the productive possibilities, and also try to surround himself with colleagues who are positive and realistic, rather than negative.

A variation on the positive, "can-do" attitude that charac-terizes many successful business people is the unwillingness to take no for an answer. I've often been tempted to go along when someone who was supposed to know told me, "You simply can't do this! . . . It won't work! . . . It's not allowed!" But on at least one important real estate deal, I thank my lucky stars that I refused to go along when I was told the deal was impossible.

Through a series of financial loans, I had ended up with a one-third interest in a 100-unit apartment building. Then, one of my partners had a bright idea: He suggested that we sell the apartment units off as condominiums, though this was a time when condominiums weren't really very well known in America.

Although the concept was new, it intrigued me, and so I went along with the proposal. But we immediately ran into a major problem. Another partner said, "We can't get any financing for these condominiums until we sell at least 50 percent of them. That's a state law!"

At first, I accepted this view, and we worked like men pos-sessed, trying to set up sales of enough of the units to meet the

50 percent requirement. We made it to over 40 percent, but we just couldn't hit 50 percent. Also, we hadn't actually *closed* the sales; we couldn't until we met that 50 percent requirement. As a result, some of the buyers we had lined up began to slip away from us, until we only had twenty remaining. During this frustrating period, we lost about a million dollars in expenses required by this project. Our outlays included loss of rent on a vacant apartment, advertising costs, interest on loans, legal expenses and management costs.

The whole situation seemed impossible—until I decided to start asking some questions. We went to our mortgage broker to get further information, and we immediately saw our mistake: There *wasn't* a state law which required 50 percent sales before loans became available! Rather, it was a policy of the mortgage brokers! A good lawyer would have prevented this costly and frustrating error.

After some intense negotiating, we convinced the mortgage broker that we should move ahead with the financing, even though we were now well short of lining up enough buyers for 50 percent of our condominium units. The mortgage brokers and banks finally understood that it was in their interest as well as ours to go ahead with the deal, and they agreed to make the money available.

We ended up not only wiping out our million-dollar loss; we also made a million. This experience of transforming the impossible into the possible, and making a lot of money in the process, caused me to go into the condominium business in a big way. We moved into thirteen states during a period in the 1960s and early 1970s when condominiums were just beginning to emerge as a major industry. Before long, we did $200 million in sales, including a $20 million project in the Georgetown area of Washington, D.C.

It was a fun, exciting, profitable and creative time. We instituted new concepts (which have since become commonplace), like carports for each apartment unit and clubhouses where members of the condominium complex could interact with one another. Also, we always gave money to the owners' association in each project to allow them to design and build the precise kind of lobby that they wanted.

As we moved into this market, many of the "experts" warned us that we didn't know what we were doing. This criticism frequently focused on our method of pricing. We'd be told, "You'll never sell those units because you're offering them at too high a price." Or "You'll never make a profit because you're selling them too low."

This was part of that old you-don't-know-what-you're-doing-and-besides-it's-impossible syndrome that I had learned to ignore. Instead of listening to the negativists or worrying about my own lack of knowledge on a given issue, I just went to the average people on the street. Invariably, within forty-eight hours after we put a condominium complex on the market, they would let us know whether we had priced the units too high or too low. They either wouldn't buy at all; or they'd buy everything so quickly that it would make the California gold rush look like a Sunday promenade. After studying the response of our buyers, we'd adjust our prices accordingly.

So it's best never to take a naysayer's word at face value. Many people simply lack the confidence and creativity to wrestle with a hard business problem until they find a solution. But if you're willing to say yes instead of no—to believe that all things are possible and that nothing is impossible—you'll be amazed at the fortunes and adventures that are waiting to reward a positive attitude.

BUSINESS PREREQUISITE #2:
A WILLINGNESS TO LOSE THE BUSINESS

Your exposure to personal risk and emotional strain tend to be greatest when you first start out as an entrepreneur. During my lifetime, I've been involved in building many companies, and so risk has become a way of life with me now. At the same time, I've learned to take steps to limit my personal risks. For example, I never give my personal guarantee to bank loans. As far as I'm concerned, nothing is worth going broke for.

But when I first started out, I had to approach new business ventures with more of an all-or-nothing approach. So I signed personally, and so, probably, will you.

Years ago, I decided to work as an independent sales representative with a chemical company in the Midwest, but I'd do it only on commission—even though I had the option to take a "draw," or regular salary. In other words, even though I was working for only one company, I was really operating as an independent entrepreneur.

The rewards were greatest that way, but so were the risks. I might have proved to be a bad rep for that particular product. Or even if I had been quite effective, there might have been no market in the area where I'd been assigned. And I might have ended up with too little income to satisfy my needs.

Fortunately, the risk proved to be worth it. I became the company's top sales rep and soon was earning more than anyone in the company except the president. But that doesn't mean this entrepreneurial way of life is right for everybody. After all, I was single and had no family responsibilities—an advantage that not every aspiring entrepreneur enjoys.

Take one man I know who's been considering starting an independent venture. He's a family man in his mid-forties with three children, two of whom are in college; and he's become fairly successful as a corporate manager. Also, he's worked hard over the past ten years to save about $50,000.

That sum was originally supposed to be a nest egg for him and his wife to fall back on, just in case something went wrong or he lost his job. Not much security, to be sure, but at least it would pay the mortgage and put food on the table for a few months. But now, an associate of his at work is trying to get him interested in starting a business which would market an educational line of toys for children.

My friend's involvement would require that he sink his entire savings into the business and also begin to put in hours after work and on weekends. His ultimate goal would be to quit his job and go into the new venture full-time within the next six months.

But he's shaky about it. He keeps doodling with figures, trying to determine how he's going to get his kids through college if he loses his shirt in this venture and finds himself without a job next year.

My advice? I told him to forget it.

There are a couple of reasons. First of all, he couldn't afford a major financial loss right now, and he knows it. Because of his family circumstances—and *not* because of some defect of character—he lacks the guts and free-wheeling abandon an entrepreneur needs to make a new venture go. He's worked so hard to save that $50,000, by doing without new cars, television sets and expensive vacations, that I don't think he could cope emotionally with a failure. He would be bearing the burden of risking his family's security as well as his own, and that would just be too much.

In short, a successful entrepreneur has to be prepared to lose *everything* and start all over again. That kind of attitude is the only thing that will give him the emotional freedom he needs to take big chances, weigh all risks logically, and keep a clear head as he makes the difficult decisions that must be made in the early stages of any new enterprise.

BUSINESS PREREQUISITE #3:
SUFFICIENT START-UP MONEY

A good rule of thumb is that it will probably cost twice as much to get a venture started as you think it will. At a minimum, you can figure you'll need 50 percent more money than you anticipate, even after the most conscientious planning and projecting.

Why should this be? Perhaps it's because all successful entrepreneurs are chronic optimists who are sure they can accomplish the impossible. So they tend to underestimate the number of types of problems they'll face. These may include the various cost overruns and inefficiencies they're bound to encounter; an unexpected lack of sales; or products that don't work properly, at least in the first stages of production.

So do some careful figuring and planning, come up with the figure you'll need to get your business off the ground—and then add 50 percent; or better still, double it. That's how much you'll probably need before your enterprise can begin to generate enough income to sustain itself.

What if you don't have this much capital?

Most beginning entrepreneurs don't. They can't convince a bank or venture capital firm to back them, and they lack the personal resources to generate the capital themselves. But as pie-in-the-sky, positive thinkers, they step out anyway, certain they can beat the odds. Fortunately, some win in spite of all the odds against them; in effect, they do the impossible. But many others quickly run into financial trouble and eventually go out of business.

Those who do make it on a shoestring may rely on periodic injections of cash from supportive family and friends. In effect, by grit and perseverance, they accomplish the impossible. You may potentially be one of these lucky, cash-poor-but-ultimately-successful entrepreneurs. So don't let anyone discourage you. You'll never know whether you can beat the odds and survive unless you try.

But here's a word of caution: If you do start out with what you know is too little cash, you'll have to pay even closer attention to some of the other ingredients that go into the successful entrepreneurial stew. Think your business strategy out very, very carefully. You can't afford to make any silly mistakes. As you operate on your shoestring, you're dangling by a thin thread that could snap at any moment.

In particular, it would be wise to consider such factors as:

- The level of support from your spouse. A spouse with an independent income can supply a financial buffer if you need some extra cash to keep the project going, or if you should happen to run short of enough money for your next meal!
- Your personal family and financial needs—can you afford to live in a cheap apartment and work sixteen hours a day for a year . . . or two . . . or three? Or do you have a couple of kids to put through college, beginning this year or next?
- The level of efficiency you've established in your business—if you're operating without a budget, you're probably finished before you even start.

BUSINESS PREREQUISITE #4: A DETERMINATION TO MAKE YOUR FIRST PRODUCT PROFITABLE

If you're working with inadequate reserves of capital, it's important to keep an eye peeled for imprudent moves every step along the way. One of the biggest traps is to decide to switch products or concepts in midstream when you begin to feel a financial pinch. Although you may think the new product will be your savior, the cost of such a switch will usually break you.

Some entrepreneurs have faced disaster when they decided to bring out an entirely new product before their first one was profitable. The problem frequently is that if the first product isn't showing a profit, either it's no good or the management is bad. Those very problems may, in turn, be perpetuated in future entrepreneurial efforts. The new products may also be poorly chosen or management mistakes may be repeated.

There was a case in which an auto dealer was in trouble, with his expenses running considerably higher than he had anticipated—largely because of poor management. Then, out of the blue, he had the opportunity to buy a second dealership at another location.

After examining this possibility for only a day or so, he quickly became convinced that this was the answer to all his problems. So he worked out a deal to take over that second location, and he began to pour a huge portion of his money and time into developing it.

That was a major—indeed, a fatal—mistake. Because of a poor understanding of proper management, he ran directly into what might be called the "second product trap"—the mistake of diverting funds and energies into a second concept before the first is managed profitably. He failed to realize that if he wasn't making money on his first dealership, the chances were very good that he'd never make it on the second one either.

That's precisely what happened. He continued to make the same errors on the second dealership that he had made on the first, and his mistakes were compounded. He started to lose money at a rapid clip in *two* business, and soon he was *out* of business.

An example like this may be depressing. Certainly, a high level of optimism and positive thinking can make the difference between success and failure. But at the same time, it's important for you to face the fact that you have to have the determination, management depth and expertise to make your first business profitable before you try to take on any extra responsibilities.

BUSINESS PREREQUISITE #5: A PRAGMATIC APPROACH TO BUSINESS AND LIFE

Entrepreneurs don't live in ivory towers. They live and operate in the real world—and they know better than most people how to take advantage of opportunities that cross their paths.

To put it another way, entrepreneurs are pragmatists who are consumed by the challenge of achieving their primary objective—a successful, profitable business. The best will subordinate almost anything, including pride and ego, to realize this goal.

One instructive example of how this pragmatism principle can operate involved my automobile dealership. I've owned that particular dealership for several decades; as a matter of fact, I had it at the time I started the rent-a-car company.

It's one of the best investments I've ever made, largely because I've been fortunate with my management. I've provided the managers with sufficient freedom and a substantial interest in the business, so they have in effect been in charge, much as they would be if they were completely on their own. As a result, we've been quite successful.

But sometimes, there are conflicts that develop—and that's where the opportunities to display the finest kind of entrepreneurial pragmatism can come to the fore.

On one occasion, for example, the manager-entrepreneur decided to change a sales program by cutting the sales commission. He planned to put the money he saved back into the advertising budget. With the resulting tripling of ad expenses, he expected that revenues and income would soar for everyone.

Having heard about what he was going to do, I was afraid of what the reaction of the sales force might be. But I decided not to step in: It's always been my philosophy to give management free rein. And there was plenty of reason for my optimism. In this case, past experience had proven the manager could exercise good, sound judgment.

In retrospect, I know now I should have cautioned him. But I decided to go with the manager because he had examined a similar approach in another state and was convinced it would work well in our dealership.

But it didn't. In fact, the entire sales organization quit, and that cost us hundreds of thousands of dollars. You can count on each salesperson, who has spent many years with a dealership, to sell about three cars a month to friends and clients, and that amounted to a loss of sixty cars a month for the twenty salesmen. Profits went through the floor; the whole thing was an unmitigated disaster.

Criticism wasn't in order because we had known beforehand and had let him move forward. Still, this incident caused us to watch the operations of that dealership more closely. Before long, another problem arose involving a serious management decision that I feared would be a disaster. This time, I decided it was necessary to step in.

So I sent in a team who told him he couldn't move in a certain direction. When he balked, they said, "Well, we're going to have to exercise the clause in the contract that allows us to buy you out."

He immediately gave in—because he's a pragmatist. This man loved the business. He knew he was perfectly suited to operate in this location. Yet he also knew that nobody's indispensable; anyone can be replaced. His very practical outlook on his work enabled him to weigh the enjoyment of his job against the needs of his ego—and give his job the priority.

This operator is a great automobile man, and a great manager. He is more willing to listen and accept other points of view, and the dealership has become even more profitable. The incident also confirmed for me that no matter how good a manager may be, there are times he's going to get off track—and those are the times that the entrepreneur-in-charge must take a strong position.

A somewhat similar lesson, though in a completely different context, can be learned from a personal encounter six or seven years ago with a leading entertainer, who happens to be a good friend of mine. He was doing some shows in Acapulco, and I had heard something about his financial difficulties. When we got together, he was very frank about his money problems, and he seemed to be looking for help.

So I said, "This is not my business, but how would you like my financial men to come in and look over your setup and make some recommendations? Maybe we could help you out on some things."

He was all for that. So our people went in and found a number of problems—such as the fact that this entertainer had borrowed $1.9 million from a bank and had failed to get one of his partners, a 50 percent owner, to co-sign the bank's loan.

First, we had the partner co-sign the bank loan, and also recommended that the entertainer sell that company. Also, my financial experts did an extensive analysis of his entire financial situation and made a number of recommendations.

Recently, when I saw him, he filled me in on what had happened since our meetings several years before. He said, "I want you to know that I followed all those recommendations. I'm in better financial shape today than I've ever been in, and I want to thank you for the help."

This internationally recognized celebrity has one of the key attributes of a successful entrepreneur: He's a thorough-going pragmatist who isn't too proud to accept help from an outsider if it seems that the proffered help will improve his business picture.

Of course, the ultimate answer to this individual's financial woes was the man himself. He has the all-important ability to *generate* large sums of money. Our recommendations about how to organize and streamline his holdings just helped him keep more of what he earned.

Yet he realized—as all of us have many times in the past—that there were some deficiencies in his business judgments. And he was quick to take action when he saw a way to make significant improvements. This readiness to change when necessary to improve profit potential is characteristic of most successful entrepreneurs.

These prerequisites reflect the basic equipment you need to make it as an entrepreneur. But it's also necessary to have an even more profound understanding about who you are and where you're going. In short, it's truly essential to know yourself, including your deepest and most intimate yearnings.

So what exactly is it you want? What does success really entail for you? What does it mean to become first in your field—and is it really worth it to seek this goal?

Five

Entrepreneurial
Hot Spots

Your Key to Becoming Number One

"My heart was hot within me, while I was musing the fire burned. . . . "

—*Psalm 39:3*

*T*he most successful entrepreneur is a person possessed by a drive to excel—and that often means beating out all the other competitors in the race. Second place simply won't do. Some persistent, gnawing voice deep inside keeps saying, "You have to sell the most . . . build the best . . . earn the 'max' . . . be the first."

Of course, few people actually make it to the very top in any field; but actually coming in first is not necessary to be successful as an entrepreneur. Rather, the key ingredient is *wanting* to be number one. This ambition will keep you going, even when everyone else is ready to quit and close up shop.

Some people seem to possess from birth an almost compulsive desire to occupy the top slot. Others acquire it. However you get this inner drive, one thing is sure: You have to have it if you hope to succeed.

Certainly, this intense kind of motivation is within the grasp of anyone reading this book. It's just a question of identifying and harnessing your "entrepreneurial hot spots"—those deep-seated, personal drives and motivations that can enable you to plow ahead, through thick and thin, until you achieve significant success.

As you know, some people want primarily to be rich. Others want power. Still others want to raise their social status. And others get enthused by the idea of improving the lot of other human beings or society in some way.

Sometimes, these driving forces may overlap in one person; other times, one motive seems to dominate. So, if you think money will solve all your problems, it may be that acquiring power or improving society won't satisfy you completely. You need the possibility of big bucks dangling in front of you to keep you going from one entrepreneurial challenge to the next. If the money isn't there, you'll soon find your business isn't much fun, and you'll run out of steam.

By the same token, if helping other people and improving society are your major needs, you'r not going to be satisfied with a multimillion-dollar enterprise or the possibility of wielding considerable power. The money and the power may be pleasant; they may even be necessary ingredients, to some extent. But by themselves, they're not going to provide you with any sort of ultimate meaning in life.

So, if you hope to succeed as an entrepreneur, you need to ride along on the crest of one or more profound inner drives in your personality. But in my opinion, you can't create or generate this sort of powerful motivation artificially. Instead, you have to look deep inside yourself and find those already-existing predilections and interests that can "set you on fire." Then, you learn to put them to work in your business ventures.

Because our lives are always a melange of mixed motives, it may take considerable introspection to discern the entrepreneurial hot spots in your own personality. But you'll surely find them—and learn to make good use of them—if you'll just take the time to search.

As I mentioned at the very beginning of this book, over the years I've learned several things about myself:

- I don't enjoy being poor—and one of the ways not to be poor is to become successful.
- I need to have control over businesses in which I'm involved.
- I get impatient and bored quite easily, so I need a variety of interests to keep me satisfied.
- I have a deep need to *create* things—things which in some way are going to improve the lot of others.

These are some of the most forceful drives that move me along through life, but which is the most powerful?

I found that after I had earned a reasonable amount of money and had become materially comfortable and financially secure, I didn't crave cash that much anymore. I didn't need a billion-dollar business empire to keep me happy. So ultimately, after a few initial successes, money receded as a major motive for me.

In more recent years, other factors have come to the fore, including a need for control, so that I could avoid unnecessary conflicts on a project; a need for variety; a need for creativity; and a need for ways to express altruism. In fact, the drives to be creative and altruistic were the most important inner impulses that pushed me to start the Avis Airlines Rent-A-Car Company. Certainly, I wanted to make money. But I also wanted to make the lives of business and vacation travelers easier and more pleasant.

At this time, I also had a very profitable automobile dealership. But quite frankly, as the airport car-rental concept gathered steam, I began to lose interest in the dealership. I even told the automobile people, "This place may be making money hand over fist—but my real interest is Avis Rent-A-Car!"

So I found a way to express those "hot spots" deep within: The concept that had the power to inspire me was an airport car-rental business, which would improve the state of the nation's transportation system. If the concept worked, it would provide an invaluable service to travelers who constantly had trouble getting out of the airports into the towns and cities where they were supposed to be enjoying a holiday or doing their business. Also, I hoped I would make plenty of money. Those factors were sufficient to build a white-hot fire under me—and the Avis car-rental company was the result.

But that's just one example of the kind of project that can inspire me to go all-out as an entrepreneur. I find that I'm highly motivated by some of the same impulses on smaller-scale ventures as well.

Take a bakery business I got into a number of years ago. Now, what do I know about baking? Not a thing. I may eat well; but making breads, pastries and other such goodies isn't exactly one of my major strengths.

In short, the nature of the business certainly wasn't the factor that prompted me to become a bakery owner. Nor was it a great desire of mine to wield power over the world's great chefs; nor some notion that succeeding with this particular bakery business could launch me on a path to billions as the baron of the world's breadbaskets.

No, my main motivation was to help a friend who had gotten into personal and financial difficulties. He owned the bakery and also was married at the time to an attractive woman who inspired him to live as a richer man than he really was. As a result he started spending a lot more money than he had—and he ended up in Chapter 11 bankruptcy proceedings.

For those of you who, happily, are not familiar with the ins and outs of the federal law, this means that he was on the verge of losing it all through bankruptcy.

At this point, my baker friend asked me to take a look at his situation, and I could immediately see that the main problem was total mismanagement. He was spending more than he could make, and he had also ended up owing the government a fortune in taxes. In addition, he owed his creditors thousands of dollars he didn't have. Part of his debts related directly to his business, and part were his personal problem.

Under the Chapter 11 rules, the baker's business was completely under the court's jurisdiction, or in "receivership," with the creditors clamoring for as much as they could get of what was owed to them. When I entered the scene during this turmoil, I first arranged to get total control of the company. This step was necessary to enable me to supply the large sums of money required and to make important corrections in management. Before long, we got everybody to agree on a repayment schedule.

Specifically, we first negotiated settlements with all the baker's creditors, and that enabled us to stop the court proceedings. But then, we hit a problem with the owner I was trying to help.

I realized that no matter how much money we gave him, he'd manage to spend more. In other words, even if I gave this man a large sum of money to leave the company, it seemed almost certain that in a couple of years he would spend it all and be broke. Then, even though I'd originally gotten into the thing because of friendship, I would be criticized for having cheated him.

So to solve this problem permanently, I decided I'd give him a very substantial salary for life. That way, he couldn't possibly go broke. Of course, he could spend all he had in hand before the next check arrived. But there would always be another check.

As a result of this plan, things worked out rather well for the baker. He was a little disturbed when his marriage broke up. But his personal finances were now in good shape; and he never had a complaint to the day he died. Just as important, we remained good friends.

As for me, I discovered there were both advantages and disadvantages to being a baker. The bakery immediately became profitable again, and my associates and I enjoyed making some fundamental improvements, such as managing the cash flow more effectively. As a result, the business expanded quite rapidly.

We even contributed a few ideas which have become a staple in a number of bakery businesses today. For example, our fast growth prompted us to develop a concept that involved putting large heaters in the warehouse which would blow into the back of the trailers during the dead of winter. These devices enabled the truckers to do their loading while their trailers were outside, and the improvement eliminated the need for a new expensive building. In the past, everyone had thought that to keep the bread warm, you had to load the bakery trailers *inside* a building.

But there were also some problems. One of the biggest was that the profit margins in the company remained lower than I liked. I knew that to increase our earnings, I'd have to get more directly involved in the company. But I simply didn't want to spend a lot of time learning the bakery business. Also, at that time I didn't know how to hire competent managers.

Also, there were perennial problems with the unions that worked for the company. One strike could have wiped out five years' profits, and the company was in no position to take that. So I decided to sell the company and move on to something else.

Unfortunately, though, when I put the bakery on the market, I discovered that a major obstacle to a sale was my original altruism in setting up my friend with a salary for life. As it happened, it was going to cost about ten times more than I thought it would to insure that salary—and it soon became clear I would have to foot the bill.

Still, even with the insured salary, when we did find a buyer, we ended up with a profit. And just as important, I had the satisfaction of knowing that I'd been able to engage in a successful entrepreneurial venture—and help a friend who probably would have lost everything.

These, then, are just a few of the things that make me tick as an entrepreneur. But how about you?

Whatever your main motive or motives in life may be, you can be sure of this: Every entrepreneurial hot spot is a double-edged sword. That is, your most basic drives have the power to push you right up to the top—*or* undercut your chances for great success. Now, let's explore the plusses and minuses of a few of the more common entrepreneurial hot spots.

HOT SPOT #1: MONEY

Money will always be a major way to measure success in business. When you talk to some business people, the first thing they want to tell you is how much they sold their company for.

Money will buy you social position, big homes, freedom to travel and the ability to put your children through the best schools. No matter how altruistic you may be, this is one of the realities of life that always confronts you. Without money, you simply cannot provide certain material advantages for your family, and you cannot go to many of the places and do many of the things you like.

Sometimes, this money motive stems from very poor circumstances as a youth. A number of entrepreneurs I know came out of very deprived backgrounds. Some didn't even know if there was going to be food on the table at the next mealtime.

One friend with this sort of early family experience told me, "Come hell or high water, I'm going to make so much money that I can't possibly be broke again."

This sort of inner drive to accumulate wealth can make you grit your teeth and shrug off all sorts of setbacks in the effort to build a successful business. But there are also some problems with the money motive.

No matter how much you have, it will never be enough. An extremely successful female entrepreneur told me, "When I was very young, I thought if I made $20,000 a year, I'd be rich. The trouble was, when I made it to $20,000, that wasn't enough. I wanted to make $30,000. Then, I had to earn $50,000."

And of course, this process never ends—even for this woman, whose companies now bring in millions. Now, she's beginning to reassess this monetary monomania that has been a major vehicle for her success. And she's beginning to realize that if money is the meaure of her success, she'll find she constantly has to keep raising her goals, as she moves past one plateau to the next. Some people drive themselves right into the cemetery trying to accumulate far more than they could ever spend or enjoy.

There are many ways to illustrate this compulsive, dark side to the drive to amass a lot of money. A friend of mine who is very rich decided to buy a jet. I asked him why he needed such an expensive thing, and he said, "If you don't have a jet, people are not going to think you're rich."

This friend had all the money in the world—and he was still worried that maybe he didn't have quite enough in the eyes of his friends! I tried to argue with him, but his mind was made up. He went out and bought that jet. But before long, the purchase failed to satisfy. Soon, he had identified some other material possession he had to have to make himself look successful.

Falling into this trap of excessive materialism can cut the heart right out of any business venture. I've known so many outstanding business people who just *had* to have that extra limousine, airplane or expense account item. Before they were even aware of it, their business was running in the red, and what had once been a promising venture had turned into failure.

So the love of money may indeed become the root of all evil for the unwary. When materialistic motives reign supreme, one thing may well lead to another, until financial disaster brings the entire venture crashing down. Some—like my baker friend with the big-spending habits—may find they can't keep even the most promising of businesses afloat.

The solution to this dilemma? If money is your hot spot, it may work well for a while. But it's always necessary to be on guard against the temptation to excessive spending. And eventually, even if you manage your finances well, you'll have to find another primary motive, or you'll end up a very dissatisfied person. Money can help, but by itself it can never bring happiness.

HOT SPOT #2: POWER

The power of building and running a thriving business has an energizing, invigorating quality that surpasses any drug known to man. But like money, power can exert a destructive as well as a constructive influence over any top executive, including an entrepreneur. In fact, power is so much like a drug that it seems to produce a kind of "withdrawal" effect when it's removed.

I was invited to attend the changing of the guard at a major American company one year, when the reins of power were passed from one chief executive officer to the next. I'll never forget that experience because the incoming and outgoing CEOs were standing right next to each other in a receiving line. The contrast between the two was stark.

One by one, other executives would pass by and say to the new executive, "It's great to see you taking over. . . . When can we play golf? . . . Can I give you a call next week?"

But they mostly ignored the outgoing CEO—and gradually, minute by minute, I could see the color drain out of his face. He had lost his power platform, and it seemed that he was becoming excruciatingly aware of it at this public gathering for the very first time. He was one of those people who later died of a broken heart.

Just as power removed can be a devastating experience, so can entrepreneurial power that spills over into one's personal life. This fact emerged as I was doing a deal with an octogenarian from New York City, who was very rich and completely wedded to his work.

As far as I could tell, this man never took a day off. Also, I was impressed, and somewhat amused, by how many of his children and other family members he had hanging around. They were accomplished, well-educated people, and included a number of lawyers and other professionals. Yet they *always* seemed to be in the office.

At one point, I jokingly asked the man, "Don't you let your family members take a vacation from the business either?"

"No," he said, without the trace of a smile. "They're just like I am. I've trained them that way. They know if they want to inherit my money, they should almost never take a day off. It's a big event when one of them leaves early in the afternoon on family or personal business."

I'm sure this man's family got some satisfaction out of working as hard as the "old man." Yet I'm also certain that he had built a successful enterprise and continued to work seven days a week, well into his eighties, largely because he had a deep need to exercise power as the family patriarch. This way of life may have given this man some satisfaction, but I question whether the cost to his family was worth the emotional price that was paid.

Exerting that kind of control over a wide range of children, grandchildren and other relatives may enhance the success of a business to some extent. But it can also get in the way of more natural, loving family relationships. I know I could never stand to work in such an environment—even if the boss were my own father and he controlled my inheritance.

HOT SPOT #3: STATUS

The drive to achieve higher status or prestige is often closely related to the need to acquire money or power. But the status motive may also be one that exists quite separately, and may arise from childhood feelings of being an outsider or inferior.

If that's the thing that moves you, there's certainly nothing wrong with it. The important thing is just to recognize it as a powerful, success-producing force and allow it to move you to new heights of financial and personal achievement.

At the same time, however, you may have to monitor and control your own feelings and reactions when your status is threatened—as it inevitably will be at some points in your business career.

One big threat to the status-conscious achiever is the fear of getting upstaged. On one occasion, the first owner of a company showed up at a party where the current chief executive officer was supposed to be the star attraction. As it happened, the former top man was something of a legend—the Founding Father of the organization who would always occupy a unique role whenever he was present at a company gathering.

Unfortunately, the current boss had a high need for premier

status, and he simply couldn't accommodate the presence of any-one who could nudge him down into second place. He tried to remain civil toward his predecessor, but he obviously was ex-tremely uncomfortable until the other man finally had to leave for another engagement.

What can a person do about such an emotional reaction? I'm not sure there is anything—other than just accepting this sort of an encounter as one of the realities of life.

There are, of course, many other entrepreneurial hot spots that may be able to build a sufficiently intense motivating fire under you. And each will undoubtedly have some negative edge that can make life miserable unless you're aware of the dangers.

One way I keep my own drives in perspective is to reflect periodically on what it really means for me to strive as an entre-preneur. During those times of self-evaluation, I frequently re-mind myself that business is just part of my life. I tend to get so intense about my projects that if I fail to ease up and relax, I could easily begin to live an excessively stressful life. And I might begin to make demands on myself and my associates which wouldn't be very healthful or beneficial for me or them.

One recent object lesson occurred as I was chatting with the owner and chairman of a company worth hundreds of millions. It was Friday afternoon, and during a break in the conversation, he called to his president, who was just passing by the open door.

The owner said, "By the way, I'm having some clients fly in tonight. Do you mind having dinner with us?"

I could tell by the look on the president's face that he *did* mind. But he replied, "Fine! That won't be any problem at all."

With such a last-minute invitation for a Friday night business dinner, it would have been a fair assumption that the company president would have had plans with his wife or family. There's no question in my mind that he called his wife and canceled his plans so that he could be at the beck and call of his boss. He knew that he could probably turn down such an invitation by the company owner once or twice. But by the third rejection, the president's job might well be in jeopardy.

That's the kind of power that a powerful business leader, or a successful entrepreneur, can wield. But it's also a power that can easily be abused. Even as the owner of a thriving business may drive himself too hard, he may also tend to do the same with his subordinates. And ultimately, all, including the business itself, will suffer.

In short, becoming number one in a field doesn't involve trampling on the sensibilities of others. Indeed, when business causes a person to reach over into his own leisure time and family life—or into those sacred areas in the lives of others—the fruits of success may suddenly turn sour.

A classic example of this involved a man I know who built a manufacturing business from nothing to a value of about $100 million. He developed a reputation as a single-minded, rather unpleasant person who was interested only in the bottom line—and not particularly concerned with his employees or colleagues as human beings.

Eventually, he sold the company, with high hopes of living out his remaining years as a retired business sage whom others would surely seek out for stimulating companionship and advice. To this end, he intended to use part of his money to buy a huge yacht. There, he planned to "hold court," with a stream of friends constantly going back and forth to his seagoing parties. That's the way he had managed his relationships in business, and he expected the same to happen in retirement.

Unfortunately, things didn't work out quite that way. He did buy an extremely luxurious vessel, which cost him several million. But the "friends" turned out to be just hangers-on, who had been mostly interested in furthering their careers through their association with him.

Other successful people visited him once or twice to see the boat. But then they started making excuses. Because he had relinquished his position of influence, he no longer had the personal pulling power to gather people around him. His personality by itself certainly wasn't warm or compelling enough to draw companions to his door.

In short, this man may have been a success on one level; he would have been considered a candidate for number one in his field by a number of tests. But in terms of his total life, he wasn't a success at all. His definition of what it means to be first had been too narrow. So his lack of a balanced life caused him to suffer a tremendous personal shock—the consequences of an un-satisfying retirement.

Certainly, there's always a price to be paid if you want to be highly successful. The long hours, constant preoccupation with your work and inevitable sacrifices in your personal life will take a toll.

For one thing, there may be significant risks for your personal relationships as you pursue projects with the single-mindedness necessary to succeed. You may also have to rely on drives and motives—like the need for money, power or status—which, by themselves, can alienate many of those who are closest to you.

So it's essential—even as you set definite goals and move ahead vigorously to achieve them—to keep in mind a broader view of what it means to be happy and satisfied in life. You have to "let up" on those fierce success drives at some point, before it's too late. If your entrepreneurial hot spots remain completely uncontrolled, they can burn you up. But if you respect their explosive energy and take steps to harness them, you'll find you're in a much stronger position to become number one—not only in your business ventures, but in your personal life as well.

Six

The Basic Secrets for Hitting the Bull's-Eye

" . . . an arrow shot from a well-experienc'd archer hits the mark his eye doth level at . . . "

—William Shakespeare, Pericles, Act I, Scene I

When I was only fourteen, I got fired from my first part-time job. Here's the way it happened:

The local sandwich and ice cream shop in my hometown had an opening for a part-time counter man, and several youngsters were really eager to get the position. The shop was one of the most popular in our neighborhood, with a great selection of sweets that drew teenagers from all over. But I got the nod over the other candidates because I seemed to have an ability to put customers at ease and sell the product.

Unfortunately, I also had a sweet tooth.

My mouth started watering the minute I put on my apron and spied the bowls of ice cream that were within easy reach. Before lunch, I had already consumed three pies à la mode.

And by the early afternoon, I was back on the street, looking for work again.

Now, you might argue that I should have known better than to raid my employer's dessert shelves that way; and I suppose there would be some merit to the criticism. But remember: I was only a kid. As I explained to my mother that night, "If they had just *told* me what was expected—that the pie à la mode cost money—I'd never have done it!"

That was true, too. Even today, I still believe that the fault lay more with the owner than with me. In fact, his problem went far beyond the way he handled one fourteen-year-old part-time employee. It went right to the heart of what it takes to be a super-successful business person.

The shop never did as well as it might have, in part because the owner periodically violated some basic principles. There are four basic steps or "secrets" involved in launching any successful business. They include: (1) deciding upon your mission; (2) setting goals that will help you realize your mission, (3) implementing those goals; and (4) following through to be sure the implementation is done properly.

Of course, these four fundamentals aren't really so secret at all—they're taught in most business schools. But many business people *act* as though they're big secrets because they repeatedly ignore or violate them. It's a shame, too, because these four elements can mean the difference between success and failure.

To see what this all means, let's consider my experience with the ice cream parlor a little more closely.

The mission of the shop's owner seemed to be to establish the most profitable and popular ice cream parlor that he could in that area.

His goals or goals—and here, I'm just making an educated guess—would have been to set up his shop on that particular corner and then to make it start paying off for him as quickly as possible. Most likely, his goals would have included achieving a reasonable level of profitability before his reservoirs of capital ran out. So, if he had set aside $10,000 to get the shop going, he would have to start making a decent income on his investment before that $10,000 had been spent.

The third basic secret of success involves the implementation of the goals, and this is where the dessert-and-sandwich man began to run into big trouble. To achieve his mission and goals, he would have had to purchase good food and prepare a high-quality menu. By most standards, he seemed to have done fairly well on this front.

But it would also have been important for him to hire a staff who could do the ice cream preparation and serve his goodies with a degree of graciousness and aplomb. Enter young Warren Avis—and what I happened to symbolize about the man's approach to implementation.

I like to think the shopowner chose well when he hired me. The process of implementation began to break down, however, in the training of the hired help. In short, my boss never bothered to tell me how a counterman was supposed to behave with the food in his care. He never said, "Don't eat the profits!"

What were the rules about eating the merchandise? How

about nibbling between meals? If you could eat the master's fare, was there any limit on quantity?

Whatever the rules were, I was never told about them. They remained unarticulated in my employer's brain; and the inexperience of youth led me to violate egregiously one of the cardinal commandments of the ice cream counterman's trade.

I recognize, of course, that at the tender young age of fourteen, I was a little short on common sense. But I've often wondered: What if I had eaten only one pie à la mode? Or were two pies the cutoff to ensure continued employment? Clearly, three were too much, but being a conscientious young fellow, I would have toed the line if I had only known what was expected.

So, despite my own shortcomings, I still conclude that the owner in this case fell short in his implementation of the mission and goals for his business. He lost some time and damaged company morale by hiring a boy who didn't work out. For one thing, the boss had to go through the interview and hiring procedure again. Also, I know for a fact that the other employees were disturbed by my firing, and their confidence in the boss's fairness and ability to communicate were shaken.

And this isn't all. The ice cream shopowner also ran into a problem with the fourth principle of entrepreneurial success—the follow-through.

Even though he made a mistake with me, he didn't learn his lesson very well. He continued to neglect training his employees and communicating to them his expectations of acceptable conduct on the job. He would punish or reprimand them after the fact—that is, after they had violated some unstated tenet of proper conduct. He apparently carried various rules and policies around in his head, but he never explained them in personal encounters, staff meetings or written instructions.

So here we have a situation where an entrepreneur had a good idea, which he expressed in the form of an exciting and promising mission. He also had worthy goals, which were well-designed to accomplish his mission. Even on the implementation and follow-through levels, he had a lot going for him: He continued to purchase tasty food for his sandwiches and desserts, and that kept a steady stream of customers passing through his doors.

But he missed the boat in other ways during his implementation. Specifically, he fell down in managing his employees and training them. So the service always left a great deal to be desired.

Furthermore, on the follow-through phase, he failed to check what was being done, to be sure it was being executed correctly. Until you develop total confidence in your employees, it helps to point out what their mistakes are, and discuss how to eliminate the mistakes.

In the final analysis, this owner achieved some success, but he never reached the heights of entrepreneurial accomplishment. For one thing, he never had the best dessert-and-sandwich shop in town. Nor did he ever become so profitable that other entrepreneurs or investors beat down his doors, trying to buy him out. Nor did he ever generate sufficient extra capital to open a second or third shop, or perhaps even a chain.

All this may seem like elementary stuff in your effort to come out a winner in the entrepreneurial game. The secrets of success may be simple on one level; at least, they're simple to state on paper. What's hard is having the discipline to carry them out.

There are four fundamentals for starting or running a business of any size. The rules are always the same, and your understanding of each of them is essential.

THE MISSION

In an entrepreneurial enterprise, the mission or purpose consists of two elements:

1. Your basic idea. This is your key concept, the essential thing you want to do. With the Avis Rent-A-Car system, my basic idea was to establish an international car rental service in airports.

2. The underlying factors or principles that will make your basic idea work. With the Avis car-rental idea, those underlying elements included: profitability; good management; efficiency; great merchandising; and excellent service.

It's important to distinguish this second element in your mission or purpose from the more specific goals you'll be setting later to enable you to accomplish your mission. We'll discuss how to set goals in more detail in the next section; for now, just remember that formulating a mission or purpose involves broader, more far-reaching statements than goal-setting.

This is where the enthusiasm—or *ecstasy*, if you will—gets generated in a new business. Every true entrepreneur begins to *soar* on the wings of a super new idea. That's what being in business is all about. Unless I sense I'm going to get a thrill out of a business concept, I know I should stay away from it.

I recently decided to begin a new company that would develop and market outstanding computerized office systems. So right at the beginning, I sat down and jotted down my mission: "Develop, market at a profit, and service the best, most streamlined office information systems in the nation."

But this is just one person talking about mission—not you, the reader. There are plenty of excellent entrepreneurs who think and operate on a more local scale, yet still make a great deal of money and enjoy a fabulous life-style while they're about it. That ice cream shopowner who hired me as a teenager was functioning on a limited basis, but that didn't matter. He could have done extremely well if only he had put his entire act together a little better.

In any case, I personally don't see any point in doing something halfway. I'm going to shoot for the moon, or not shoot at all! I think most entrepreneurs are like this. You first come up with an idea; and then you wonder, consciously or subconsciously, "How can I get the most mileage, money and ultimate meaning in life out of this concept?"

People constantly raise questions about this beginning stage of a venture. They're especially fascinated by ideas. They'll wonder: "How do you come up with ideas for a new business? Also, when you do get an idea, how can you tell whether or not it's likely to be a success? And how do you 'shape' an idea so that it's positioned to generate maximum success and profits?"

There are a number of ways to come up with ideas. First of all, always keep a little "idea book." Any business person who doesn't jot down ideas is going to forget a certain percentage of them. And that idea that slips your mind may be the very one that could have been your key to great success. So don't take any chances! Write them all down!

Then, when you have a little spare time, go back over the thoughts you've written down and select those that seem to have the most potential. At the same time, begin to play with the best items, trying to mold them into a form that seems most rewarding and profitable.

But that still leaves the question: Where do entrepreneurial ideas come from?

Ideas for businesses form when there's a *need*—and it's usually a very personal thing.

As we've seen, that's how the Avis airport car-rental system got started. Clearly, there was a crying need for some sort of automobile transportation in airports for travelers. That was where my idea began.

Gradually, my entrepreneurial mission came into focus. In short, I was going to set up an airport car-rental business which would:

- Fill a need that had never been filled before;
- Involve the creation of something entirely new in the field of private transportation;
- Make a significant contribution to society by making life much easier for hundreds of thousands of travelers; and
- Generate a great deal of money.

Sound familiar? Although that was a rather complete statement of my mission for this airport car-rental enterprise, it's also interesting that the mission coincided in many ways with my own "entrepreneurial hot spots," which I described in the previous chapter. Our best ideas—and business missions which are based on those ideas—most often spring out of our deepest personal motivations and interests.

The same sort of thought and emotion went into the idea of developing the nation's best computerized office information system. I've never had time for day-to-day management of companies; yet it's also always bothered me that my lack of time made me vulnerable in that area.

But then the potential of using high-tech concepts to manage more effectively with less effort started to catch my fancy a few years ago. So I resolved to get stronger in this area by applying my fascination with high-tech to the daily operations of a business. One result has been the computerized office systems company mentioned earlier, which I hope will make a significant contribution to upgrading and streamlining the nation's office systems.

It's easy to get a misleading, simplistic impression about getting ideas. An idea, whether it comes from a painter, a novelist or a business person, is the result of creativity. And creativity takes time. You have to have time—often, a busy person must *make* time—to allow an idea to work itself out. It you're always busy working at your job, you're simply not going to be creative. That's why idea-oriented people, from the ancient Greeks to many modern professors, always try to make sure they have plenty of time just to think.

This means setting aside the time, or structuring a period for creativity regularly into your life. In part, this time for creative thinking and meditation is a time to clear your mind.

The Japanese have traditionally set aside times for meditation; so have those from other spiritual backgrounds. There's a recognition in these traditions that an important part of life, and perhaps the most important part, transcends our daily existence. But if you're constantly working on the problem at hand, you'll never be able to detach yourself from it, evaluate it and be able to come up with a new and more creative solution. Similarly, you'll never be able to rise above your present problem and enter into another dimension of thought where you can see in a completely different way some ordinary thing that usually escapes your attention.

Even when walking through the park, I try to be observant about the things around me. I might be figuring how to make the park more beautiful. Or in strolling down Fifth Avenue in New York City, I may be musing about how to improve the congested traffic. Even while relaxing out on a farm, I may be considering a different way to arrange the fences or shrubs to get more productivity or beauty out of the land.

For a concrete illustration of how this idea-generating mechanism works, consider this approach to a couple of pieces of property of mine—a farm and also a private home. In both places,

I'm experimenting with an underground watering system. Of course, this concept didn't spring full-blown into my brain, with no mental preliminaries whatsoever. It's crystallized step-by-step in my thinking, and the mental process is still in the works.

The idea about improving the watering system originally began because I got tired of seeing the grass burned up in our green areas. Most sprinkling setups are troublesome and inefficient; consequently, practically everybody has a problem watering grass.

Sprinkler systems are always breaking down: Either they don't work at all, or they put out too much water. The result is that the grass doesn't grow right. The sun burns it up, or the roots don't reach down into the ground far enough. In many cases, the roots may have to grow back up toward the surface to get to the water; the grass doesn't root well; and finally, it begins to die.

As I mused on this problem, I perceived a real need—a need which stretched well beyond my own private sphere. It became evident to me after much research that a better way to water our extensive grassy areas would be to water them from below the ground.

The main idea, which was originally developed by others, has been to take a plastic pipe with holes in it, implant it in the ground and then water the roots of the plants and grass instead of their tops. By using this method, you can encourage the roots to go down to the soil and thereby strengthen the grass and plants. You also use only about a tenth of the water required by a regular watering system. And you don't burn up the plants either.

We tested this approach extensively, and we made plenty of mistakes. First, we couldn't figure out how deep to put the pipes into the ground, and also we had trouble determining the right amount of water to use, even though the original developers gave us guidelines. In short, we've made plenty of blunders trying to see if it was a viable product.

I'm fairly sure now that even if it works well for us, we'll never go beyond the point of using this system on a purely personal level. Among other things, there are a number of problems in merchandising it to a wider public. Also, the servicing is very expensive. But this sort of testing is just part of the way we do a feasibility study.

If we ever get to the point where we decide to set up a

company and sell a product, then we'll already have our mission pretty well formulated. The mission phase of launching an entrepreneurial venture is completed after you fine-tune your basic idea and then state it as a basic business objective or purpose. So, with the watering system, we would want a national company that would be highly profitable with the best service and cost-effective methods for growing grass.

Finally, settling on a mission isn't usually up to just one individual. Even if you're the head honcho who has started the business, put up the money and generally taken charge of the whole shebang, you have to be sure that those who are working closely with you are generally in agreement with your vision. Otherwise, you may fail.

In fact, getting the entire staff on board when formulating a mission is very important. So encourage everybody to participate! Sit them all down and ask them to write down what they see as the basic mission of the company. There will be many variations of the mission. But usually, they'll all agree enthusiastically on the basic business objectives and contribute many worthwhile suggestions for improving the understanding of the mission or purpose.

It isn't just agreement you're looking for. Rather, by having an opportunity to sit down and think about the direction of the company, you start out with people who are more likely to be more effective and productive in realizing the ultimate mission. They understand the mission; they help write it; and therefore they become more committed to it because they are part of it. As a result, they require fewer meetings and are more effective as they move to accomplish the mission.

This process of getting some sort of consensus about the mission is absolutely essential, especially as you deal with employees, partners or shareholders. In one company, two men formed a partnership to produce a business information publication. In many ways, it was a good idea because they both had considerable experience and excellent credentials. But there was a fatal flaw—one which centered on their different views of the mission.

The problem was that the mission of one of the men was to use the business as a steppingstone to build a major financial empire. He wanted maximum profit and was ready to cut anything that didn't produce a profit. The other's mission, in contrast, was primarily to establish a top-drawer advisory service for average, individual investors who were not getting adequate advice from other professional sources. Profit wasn't that important to him; spending to improve the quality and scope of the newsletter was.

Of course, these two men had a clear-cut conflict in their concepts of the mission. It may seem that a divergence in objectives could be glossed over in the day-to-day operations of such a business. But that's rarely the case. Usually, the final result will be conflict, lawsuits and failure.

In this particular situation, the man who was primarily interested in building a quality service for individual investors was willing to spare no expense to achieve his objective. He would place phone calls to any spot in the world; hop on an airplane at the drop of a hat to pursue a story; or hire platinum-plated financial writers whenever that seemed the best way to get the goods for an article.

In contrast, his partner, who mainly wanted a financial empire, was mostly concerned with the bottom line. So he was always pressing to cut back on editorial expenses. Also instead of editorial excellence, he emphasized money-making sidelines, like seminars with some commercial angle or advertising inserts which the other partner regarded as merely peripheral.

As a result of this conflict in their understanding of their mission, these two men simply couldn't get along. Almost every day, they disagreed violently on some set of expenses—because their mission and goals were in conflict. They didn't have a chance to succeed. They regularly ran into impasses in trying to make decisions. Without a clearly defined, agreed-upon understanding of their basic business purpose their relationship degenerated into constant fights—and eventually, failure.

The publication soon went under and the two partners parted ways, considerably wiser about the need for reaching an agreement on mission, and for setting mutually agreeable goals necessary to achieve the mission.

An accurate statement of your mission, then—and some consensus among co-workers—is an absolutely essential first step in launching a successful venture. Without having your statement of mission accepted by your people (and partners), you can't even consider setting goals. In fact, it's impossible to set goals without an agreed-upon mission or purpose.

THE GOALS

Goals involve a statement of the way that you and your people plan to accomplish your basic mission.

Most people try to set their goals before they ever get their mission or purpose in focus. Consequently, they get off to false starts and find their efforts and energies are scattered and in conflict—because they've never really settled on their basic direction. So mission must come first. It's simply a matter of being systematic.

To illustrate the relationship between mission and goals, let's return to a company mentioned before—the one involving computerized office information systems. You'll recall that the basic mission of that company, which is called Avis Management Systems, was to come up with the best office information system in existence—including top-notch hardware, software, "networking" and training programs. Also, we wanted to market it at a profit on a national basis, with the best possible service organization backing it up.

That was just the basic mission, but what about the goals? The goals must get much more specific than the mission because they establish the specific targets that we have to shoot at to achieve that mission.

In a way, you might say that setting goals is a way of identifying the bull's-eyes of your mission. After you've stated your mission, if you can just identify the right bull's-eyes (goals) and put yourself in a favorable position to hit them, you're well on your way to big success. All that remains, as we'll see shortly, is the very important implementation and follow-through to realize the mission and goals.

One major goal in developing an effective computerized information system with Avis Management Systems was to come up with the best possible detailed "chart of accounts." That was a key bull's-eye we wanted to hit. In case you're not an expert in accounting or bookkeeping, a chart of accounts is simply a precise breakdown of how you plan to separate and keep track of certain items in your books. That way, with little effort or cost, you can use detailed, computer-generated spread sheets to keep tight control over costs and to facilitate forecasting.

Suppose, for instance, you incur expenses related to your company automobile. In your chart of accounts, you would want to "break out" such things as the insurance costs; so you'd set up an insurance entry with a separate chart-of-accounts number attached. Then, when an invoice comes in for car insurance, you would know where to enter it in your computer so it would be with the car insurance expense items.

Of course, our goal with Avis Management Systems has been to get much more detailed in everything. Where a typical company might have one account for an item of expense or income, we might have five separate categories. The idea is to "break out" every detail needed for spread-sheet cost analysis.

Many companies might provide one ledger line to cover all their auto expenses. But we'd have several categories. For each car, we'd include interest payments, insurance, taxes, the cost of gasoline and oil per mile, outlays for repairs, and a variety of other items related to each car. We also have our chart of accounts set up so that we can give you a computer spread sheet which will indicate whether you should keep the car, trade it in for a new one or perhaps rent instead of own.

In many businesses, company cars tend to cost much more than managers think they are costing. And those costs are probably distributed in ways the owner is only vaguely aware of. So, our chart of accounts might reveal that because you're spending a small fortune on repairs, you should buy a new car. In any case, you can only make an intelligent decision when you can compare precise costs with a computer spread sheet in front of you.

That's what Avis Management Systems is all about. A major goal was to devise the most comprehensive and accurate chart of accounts possible. Then, the implementation of that goal would involve field-testing the chart of accounts—fine-tuning and tailoring it so that it would work well on standard computer programs with a variety of companies.

You'll also recall that part of the mission with Avis Management Systems was to come up with a *national* office information system. That means we have to have some goals about how to go national: Should we hit New York and Los Angeles first? Or should we go for some smaller cities in other parts of the country and then try the big metropolitan areas on the two coasts after we've made progress elsewhere? You make these decisions as you set goals designed to reach your mission of going national.

These decisions we're making and goals we're setting are business "bull's-eyes," or goals, that *must* be identified before moving on to the next phase of implementing goals. You'll always hear people telling you that you can't possibly succeed in anything unless you set goals—and that's absolutely correct. But many people often fail to set the mission. It's important always to understand how goals relate to your basic statement of mission, and goals cannot be set without a clear-cut mission. A proper set of goals is a natural outgrowth of the mission or purpose, and the two must always be considered together, in tandem. Goals won't help you one whit if they aren't consistent with your basic mission or purpose.

In short, your mission sets the general direction toward which your energies must be directed. Your goals define the relevant bull's-eyes. If you begin to shoot for things on the wrong rifle range, you may land squarely in the center—and yet come up with a score of zero. So always remember to keep your basic mission in mind as you go through the process of goal-setting.

THE IMPLEMENTATION

Now, we come to the tough part. The attempt to implement mission and goals is the point where the breakdown in a new business usually occurs. If you've set your mission and goals properly, a venture may still fall apart in the final two steps—implementation and follow-through. Of the two, the implementation phase is by far the more difficult.

It's at this point that you get into the slogging, day-to-day operations of a company. You form your management teams; then, as they begin to delegate authority, they rely on those subordinates who have worked on the mission and goals to grasp and execute the company vision of the mission and goals. You also expect your people to begin to move during implementation toward the goals which they've helped set. Often, if the mission and goals weren't developed properly, with consensus decision making and extensive discussions, unresolved conflicts will begin to emerge during implementation—conflicts which should have been solved during discussions of mission and goals.

As the months and years pass on and the operations get more complex and mundane, the initial excitement will inevitably wear off. It's also inevitable that some people will become disenchanted and frustrated when things aren't working well, and the morale of the entire company may be jeopardized.

In one venture, which produces a high-tech device designed to transmit office information at lightning-fast speeds, the statement of mission and setting of goals were right on target. But then, they began to run into problems in the implementation phase.

I had been extremely impressed with the young man in charge, and was convinced he was completely competent to make the operation go. He was full of ideas, highly intelligent and had a unique ability to inspire those under him.

Unfortunately, too much faith was put in those qualities without checking his other management skills or his backup management team. So I had only myself to blame when I walked through those company doors and discovered the things that were going wrong.

At the very beginning, the company seemed to be doing rather well, at least on paper. The profits were rolling in, and at first, I didn't think my presence was all that important. My attitude has always been: If it's doing well, don't mess with it! Even if the young manager made $1.5 million in blunders while learning the ropes the first year, it really didn't matter so long as he was able to earn the projected $5 million. And that seemed quite possible because of the highly technical, highly profitable product he and his young team had developed.

The real trouble occurred when the company hit an early blip in sales. The earnings dropped precipitously; and the lack of experienced management and expense control nearly put the company out of business.

We discovered unbelievable things going on when I commenced my belated visits to the organization. Here's a sampling: They had given one employee, who was making $20,000 a year, a $20,000-a-year raise. Also, a young fellow with no experience had been chosen to head the production department. He had proceeded to put nearly a half-million dollars' worth of the machines we were selling on the shelf because he didn't have the experience to repair them. Also, he lacked the expertise to check errors and make corrections during production.

Now, I realize I have to assume most of the blame for such mismanagement. I was the major stockholder, and I know what it takes to implement any given mission and set of goals. As I said, if it's running well, don't mess with it—only in this case, it wasn't running so well!

One of the major things they lacked in this organization was people with experience—some gray hair. Certainly, the young people who had been brought on staff were very bright. But they had no background or experience in the areas of management—including production, service and finances—that were hurting the company the most.

Take the production manager. Getting a good production person is somewhat like getting a good doctor. You don't go to somebody who has just finished medical school if you've been scheduled for major surgery. If you're going to be cut up on that operating table, you want someone who has received a top-flight degree and also has years of experience. Others have probably died as they've given a new surgeon a chance to learn his craft. Similarly, the production department in a manufacturing company needs a manager with experience and training to be effective.

Luckily, we noticed our problems with this business in time—though I must admit that my first reaction was, typically, to be impatient. I wanted to say, "Forget it! Merge it with another company! Sell it! I don't want to be bothered with it!"

But then I got more rational. We hired a consultant at $8,000 a month to work with the company president until he could get his feet on the ground.

As it happened, bringing in the consultant was just the thing we needed. In working out a proper implementation that would help us fulfill our mission and meet our goals, he began to set up weekly meetings for the top management. Few had been held before: If you can believe it, they were so busy doing their thing, they weren't communicating with one another! Opportunities to exchange advice and provide feedback were practically nil.

The consultant also did extensive interviews within the company to determine who should remain on the job, and who was hopelessly out of his league. In addition, this man handled the hiring for some new top management people, including a comptroller and production manager.

Proper implementation, then, is just a matter of getting down in the trenches and making sure that every detail in your new company is working to meet the goals that have been set to accomplish the mission. You have to be present; you have to be observant; and you have to be diligent in this phase. It's at this point that the need for your most extensive work—the twelve-, fourteen- and sixteen-hour days—comes into play.

Implementation isn't the most inspiring or glamorous part of a business venture. But it's the firmest foundation for ultimate success as you strive to realize your goals and mission.

THE FOLLOW-THROUGH

The fourth and final phase of any business venture, the follow-through, is also a sine qua non for a successful venture. The last two phases often merge almost imperceptibly into one another because effective follow-through is merely the logical extension of proper implementation. The main idea with follow-through is to keep things working properly. It's like a regular medical check-up—bothersome but necessary.

So, in the example that we just discussed—involving the manufacturing company which was producing the high-tech office information device—implementation was improved by hiring a consultant who could correct the management problems. But the implementation could still have fallen apart if management hadn't continued to follow-through, and follow-through again. That involved checking and re-checking how the implementation was going—a process that's necessary until you have total confidence in the people and organization you're working with. Periodic monthly reviews are necessary or serious failures will develop.

Also, follow-through is essential in helping you learn from your mistakes. Unsolved failures are those that lack sufficient follow-through to find the failure.

So, things may be moving along well right now, but what about six months from now? A year from now? Or two years into the future? You need follow-through to keep evaluating and adjusting as things change if you hope to maximize your business potential.

In other words, you may put yourself on solid ground and begin to show a profit almost immediately. But then if you slip back into bad habits, because of a failure to follow-through, all of your initial efforts at setting mission and goals, and at implementation may have been in vain. You'll merely postpone an inevitable disaster to some point in the future, when it will cost many times more than the cost of follow-through in lost hard cash and customer goodwill.

As we've already seen, one of the biggest blunders that I ever made in this area was with the Avis Rent-A-Car system. I guess I'm a trusting soul because I never imagined that people would try to cheat if they were making lots of money. But I found out differently at one point when I *failed to follow-through* with audits on one phase of our operations.

In particular, when setting up our licensees in airports all around the country to run our car-rental outlets, we decided not to do any extensive checkups on the revenues they were reporting. In retrospect, I shudder to think how trusting I was because these revenue reports were the basis for calculating the fees the licensees owed.

The problem of follow-through in this case became apparent when I decided to cut corners a little too sharply on my expenses. I determined that I just couldn't afford to hire auditors to run all over the country checking licensees—in other words, to follow-through on our far-flung operations. Also, I trusted everybody. What a lesson I learned!

Unfortunately, it turned out later that a number of the licensees were stealing us blind. They would report lower revenues than they were actually receiving. Later, after I sold out, Avis set up a more extensive audit procedure than I had originally instituted, and many licensee fees went up accordingly.

It was a costly error. We had implemented the audit procedures; but obviously, we had failed to follow-through. So I ultimately had to pay a heavy price.

These four steps, then, are the "secrets" for hitting the bull's-eye of success in your business. It's helpful to think of them in terms of firing a weapon:

The mission involves getting your basic purpose or objective into focus with your team of workers—or being sure you know what "rifle range" you're supposed to be on and the general direction you're supposed to be firing.

The goals are the specific targets you're shooting for in trying to accomplish your mission. They have to be firmly fixed; if your goals keep moving about, you're sure to miss them. You want to be able to put your rounds into the center of every chosen target, every time. That's the way to achieve maximum success.

If you're going to have the best chance of hitting the center of your goal, you have to be sure that you're well trained in implementation and that your weapon is in proper working order: It should be well oiled, spanking clean and adjusted for the right windage and elevation. Now, you're well into the implementation.

If you're going to become an enduring champion, month after month and year after year, follow-through becomes essential. You have to continue to pay attention to the condition of your weapon, the effectiveness of your practice sessions and your mental preparedness. Failing to check key procedures may lower your score.

So when you're actually on the firing line, blasting away, you focus on the proper stance, proper breathing and a steady squeeze, round after round, day in and day out. The same principles apply in business. This is the secret of follow-through.

Seven

Something Ventured, Everything Gained

"Money is the seed of money, and the first guinea is sometimes more difficult to acquire than the second million."

—Jean Jacques Rousseau,
A Discourse on Political Economy

*I*f you need money for your business—and every business person I know does—there are at least three ways to get it.

First, for a start-up company you can employ what is called "nickel-dime financing"—or pulling in relatively small sums here and there from friends and family members. When you're operating on a shoestring, without one large comfortable sum to nurse your enterprise along until it becomes profitable, you often have to cut corners everywhere to make ends meet. So this approach may entail living at a near-starvation level in order to free as many personal funds as possible for the business venture.

This nickel-dime technique is certainly a hard, nerve-racking way to go. But sometimes it's the only choice that a newcomer may have.

The second way to generate start-up capital for a new business is to go to a bank—and the next chapter will focus on some of the difficulties and pitfalls with this approach.

The third way to get seed money for a new enterprise is to go to a "venture capitalist." In this case, the money will come from private, non-bank sources—such as well-heeled individuals, other corporations or limited partnerships that specialize in supporting new business concepts.

One major advantage of dealing with a venture capital firm is that you're likely to get more money than a bank will provide—without having to pay exorbitant interest rates. In fact, it's likely you won't have to pay any interest at all.

Sound too good to believe? Well, there is a catch: Even though you may not have to pay interest, you probably will have to give up a piece of your company. In recent years, in fact, venture capitalists are often taking as much as 50 percent or more of a company. Furthermore, they may also require a great deal of say in how the entrepreneurial operation is run. Why insist on such control? Venture capitalists have learned some hard lessons as they've backed extremely bright people without enough business knowledge.

Now, this may seem a big price to pay for enough up-front capital to get your money-making idea off the ground. But with a venture capitalist in your corner, you're much more likely in the long run to weight the odds in your favor and turn your concept into a significant success. One-half of a profitable company is always better than total ownership of a loser. Or as entertainer Art Linkletter has said about some of his own entrepreneurial ventures: "I've learned that it's always better to have a small percentage of a big success, than a hundred percent of nothing."

In "venture capital adventures," I've learned the hard way that we must always require some control over new companies we back. Specifically, we include a condition that will allow us to take over the management of a new company if things start going haywire.

This lesson came home to me when I took a major position in a company with a great high-tech product which I was certain would sell very well. The concept involved a gamble—I knew that. But I'm a risk-taker; and besides, I thought there was a good chance that the product would be successful. Sure enough, there turned out to be great demand for it.

Unfortunately, however, as usually happens, the management of the company miscalculated the cost of getting its product accepted by customers in the field. As a result, they ran out of money much sooner than they had expected and were on the verge of extremely serious financial problems. But even in these straits, the youthful head of the enterprise wanted to forge ahead on his own, without any management advice.

It was at this point that I realized the serious mistake I had made. I had failed to negotiate a provision in our contract with this company that if they failed to meet certain goals in their business plan, the management would revert to our venture capital organization.

In short, I had been too much of a starry-eyed optimist. I simply didn't think there would be a problem; but I've since learned that there often *is* a problem.

Fortunately, this story has a happy ending. At first, as I've said, the management of the new company plowed ahead on their self-destruct course, hoping against all reason and evidence that the product would sell at a high enough volume that they would be able to recoup their losses. But of course, that turned out to be just wishful thinking.

Soon, mismanagement on several levels began to cause the company to sink. All the while, we remained on the sidelines, gritting our teeth, to be sure—but also patiently and gently prodding managers in the directions we felt they should be going. And finally, they began to listen. Today, this company is doing quite well because they've begun to follow the management guidelines which had been suggested all along.

Although we came out of this difficult situation with flying colors, I intend never to get boxed into such a position again. I won't agree to put up money for any sort of entrepreneurial adventure without insisting on some degree of management control. There are just too many headaches that are counterproductive. Most other venture capitalists these days feel the same way.

This attitude, by the way, doesn't reflect a desire by venture capitalists to take advantage of impecunious entrepreneurs. Rather, it's just good common sense. An experienced venture capital outfit simply tends to know more about establishing and running a successful start-up company than a young, first-time entrepreneur.

Nor is this desire for management influence by venture capitalists limited to start-up enterprises. Before they put up their money, private financiers may also want some control over a troubled venture which is already well under way. Usually, such a business has begun to run into serious difficulties because of management difficulties.

This happened with another manufacturing company which was on the brink of financial disaster. A distributing company that we owned was doing a large amount of business with this particular manufacturing company. But then delays began to occur in the shipments of the manufactured product to our distributor, and we began to wonder what was going on.

After doing a little investigation, we discovered that the manufacturing company, through a variety of types of mismanagement, had started getting far overdue on many of its accounts payable. They owed enormous bills, and the squeeze these debts were putting on their cash flow had endangered millions of dollars in their sales.

The manufacturing company, knowing that we were involved in venture capital projects, came to us and explained their problem. It became clear, however, that what they wanted most was to get a big chunk of money from us and then immediately pay off all their debts.

Now, this proposal may sound nice and logical. But there was a great deal more involved than simply bailing out a manufacturer with cash problems. Certainly, the company's product had become important to our own distributing business, and it would be in our best interests to get them back on their feet as soon as possible. But underlying the whole issue was a business relationship we needed to cultivate, and that consideration went far beyond any immediate concern with company debts.

Several sticky issues were involved: First of all, there was the perennial problem of the extent to which we should exercise management control over a company. Because this manufacturing company had become a going-concern without our help, it would have been unwise to negotiate a management takeover.

On the other hand, it didn't make a lot of sense to us to take them up on their proposal that we just assume a Santa Claus role. If we had simply handed them money to pay off their debts with no strings attached, that would still have left several important questions unanswered.

One of our concerns was that it was very important for us to maintain an ongoing business relationship with this manufacturer. As I've indicated, our distributing company did a great deal of business with the troubled manufacturer. So if they had used our money to get out of debt and then taken their product to another distributor, that would have reduced our distributor's business.

You may object, "But isn't that being awfully suspicious— to think that another company would be so ungrateful as to take your money and then drop you for somebody else?"

And at first glance, it may seem like unwarranted paranoia. But believe me, there were some good reasons for our fears.

For one thing, it would be unbusinesslike for any venture capitalist to give another company a large sum of money with no conditions on the use of that money. There has to be some sort of responsibility and obligation attached to any contribution of capital. Otherwise, the recipient will have no incentive to change the poor business practices that got the company into its financial difficulties in the first place. It will just be a matter of time before the company gets right back into trouble again.

Also, there was a specific difficulty that we faced in this situation. It's true that our distributing company was doing a lot of business with the financially strapped manufacturer. But we also were acting as distributor for another product from an unrelated company which was in competition with this manufacturer.

So you can see the problem we faced: If we had given the first manufacturer a large amount of money with no conditions, they might very well have said at some point in the future: "Sure, we got some money from you. But you've been violating our trust by dealing with a competitor. So we don't feel bound to continue doing business with you."

When money is involved, it's all too easy to come up with rationalizations for changing the rules.

So what was the solution to this sticky wicket?

There was really only one responsible course of action we could take: We notified the troubled manufacturer that there was no way we would pay off all their debts immediately: "You've let this financial problem run on for some time, and we simply can't be the white knight in this situation."

At the same time, however, we emphasized that we were sympathetic with them, and also we were extremely concerned about seeing them get back on their feet. The best way of doing this, we said, seemed to be *not* to play Santa Claus with them with a one-time gift. Rather, we wanted to set up an ongoing working relationship. That way, we could protect our own interests and at the same time help them overcome their debt problems.

Specifically, we worked out a very precise program whereby we would give them money in regular increments to pay off all their delinquent bills. We also agreed to provide them with an extra influx of cash to help them keep their accounts current. In return, they agreed to continue doing business with us well into the future.

As a result of this arrangement, we got more deeply involved in influencing the management and marketing strategies—but without threatening their identity as an independent organization. They consulted us about their future sales projections, and we in turn listened closely to them about their ideas for increasing our ability to penetrate the market with greater sales of their product. Because we were tied together financially, there was a sense on both sides that "we're all in this thing together."

The final result? Trust levels between our companies were strengthened; the financial problems of the manufacturer disappeared; and the potential for greater profits on both sides soared.

So these are just a few of the things that a venture capital company can do for you. But how do you go about finding one?

It's relatively easy to find the names, addresses and telephone numbers of venture capitalists. If you check with an accountant or lawyer, or go to one of the entrepreneurial magazines such as *Venture* magazine, you'll find enough possibilities to get you started.

But in some ways this is putting the cart before the horse. You'll be wasting your time trying to contact a venture capitalist unless you have all of your "tin soldiers" lined up in the proper order. In other words, you've got to be prepared to persuade a venture capitalist before you set up a meeting. And the most powerful tool at your disposal will be a business plan, or "pro forma" as it's sometimes called.

THE ENTREPRENEUR'S MASTER KEY TO MONEY POWER: THE BUSINESS PLAN

Before you ask any knowledgeable person or organization for money—and that includes venture capitalists, banks or any other financial source—you'll have to write up a comprehensive and convincing business plan.

In brief, a business plan is a detailed summary of why you feel your proposed idea or product is going to be profitable. Most important of all, your plan should be a statement about why somebody else should put up capital for your concept.

The best business plans will begin with a clear, compelling summary of what your product is and where you expect it to go. It's important to get your prospective money people excited right at the outset. If you bore them or confuse them in the first few pages of your proposal, they're not going to be eager to give you access to their funds.

After you get your possible financial backer interested in the introduction to your plan, you've got to give him something solid. Any venture capitalist or banker with even a modicum of experience is going to see through excessive hype, so it's necessary to provide solid information as soon as possible.

For one thing, you'll need to describe your product in great detail. Don't worry too much about inundating a prospective backer with too much engineering information. He'll probably be considerably more knowledgeable than you might expect in technical areas; and if he's not, he'll have access to experts who are.

You'll also want to map out the specifics of your marketing strategy and compare your product and approach with what other companies in the field are doing.

Then, you'll have to get into the numbers. It's at this point that a good accountant becomes invaluable. Every business plan includes projected profit-and-loss statements and goes into great detail on expected expenses and income at different stages of the projected development of the enterprise.

Such financial projections are essential to any business plan, in part because they force the entrepreneur to think through realistically, on paper, how much money his proposed concept may be able to generate. I must admit, though, that I personally don't put a great deal of stock in pro forma projections. I know from experience that entrepreneurs and their accounting people can come up with almost any kind of figures—especially if they're operating out of a lack of experience or an excess of optimism.

On the other hand, there are certain features of any business plan that we look at very closely, in part because of experience in starting up companies and understanding likely pitfalls. Also, we've become sensitive to certain factors as a result of computerized models that we've devised for locating errors in venture capital projects.

In most companies, for example, there are two factors that we give the most attention to at the outset. Those are: (1) the feasibility or market potential of the product, and (2) the quality of the company's management.

These two ingredients are the "name of the game" for new or established ventures. If you've got a good product at the right price and good management, then you're going to make money. If you lack either the product or the management, your chances of success are limited.

In the last analysis, a business plan (or pro forma) is never cast in concrete. It can't possibly tell you for certain what will happen. The most a plan can do is give you certain guideposts that can be an aid to predicting what *might* happen.

Also, the business plan can tell the venture capitalist something about the business sense of the entrepreneur.* Many would-be entrepreneurs are simply "blue-sky" types. That is, they're great at coming up with tantalizing ideas and fantasizing about them. But they don't have the nuts-and-bolts knowledge that's necessary to turn a great idea into a significant profit.

But if you have a good idea . . . your product is attractive . . . you can produce it for a reasonable amount of money . . . you've assembled a competent management team . . . and you've put together the best possible business plan you can devise—*then* you're ready!

Now, one other word on the control that venture capitalists may demand: If your proposal encourages them to offer a large amount of their money for a start-up project, you can be sure they'll want to take a sizable amount from your control of the company. And most likely, you'll have to concede something on this point.

But you should still be able to retain significant control *if* you can keep a healthy momentum in your growth and meet

---

* See the Appendix for more detail on this subject.

certain preestablished goals, which are agreeable to the venture capitalist. In other words, ask for a clause in your contract that will allow you to retain control if you maintain a certain level of performance.

Most venture capitalists prefer not to get involved in the management of a company they have invested in unless it's absolutely necessary. If an entrepreneur's management system falls apart or his financial soundness falters, it will take considerable time, money and effort for the venture capitalist to put things back in order. That definitely means doing more than slapping together a short business plan during an hour or so one evening. If you try that, you certainly won't have much chance of getting support from an experienced venture capitalist.

Certainly, the venture capitalist would probably rather get involved than lose his investment. But in the best of all possible worlds, he'd much prefer to put his money into a new company, take a percentage of the ownership and profits, and sit back and watch the company succeed. Unfortunately, however, in the real world this perfect-profit scenario may not work out in quite such rosy terms. So certain safeguards have to be built in to protect both the entrepreneur and the venture capitalist.

But of course, the venture capital route is not the only way to go to get financing. Family or friends may be able to help out, though this approach usually leaves you short of the cash you really need. Many entrepreneurs also turn to the most traditional and conservative source of funds—their local banks. And if they follow certain simple principles, they can make use of bank loans rather successfully.

Eight

Is There Any Such Thing as a Friendly Banker?

"Bankers are just like anybody else, except richer."

—*Ogden Nash*, I'm a Stranger Here Myself.
I Have It on Good Authority.

Among many aspiring entrepreneurs there's a popular set of notions about money that goes something like this:

To ensure success, it's necessary to have a lot of money "up front," or at the very beginning of the venture.

Big bucks come only from banks.

But banks are notoriously hostile to new business ventures—especially with fledgling entrepreneurs who don't have a track record.

So why bother? You're usually going to be defeated financially before you even get started!

There's a grain of truth in each of these four points; but there's also a great deal that's misleading. In fact, banks and bankers that understand start-up companies can be quite helpful to those entrepreneurs who know how to approach them properly.

My encounters with the banking industry have covered a lot of ground and go back a long way. There was a time that I actually *bought* control of a bank.

I had done a study of prospective businesses in a fast-growing community and became enthusiastic about the possibility of owning what looked like a bank with real possibilities. So we began to negotiate for the purchase of the organization, and while I was on a trip to Europe the sale went through.

When I returned from Europe I found that a board meeting of the bank's directors had been called and I was the new chairman. It was a great feeling; instead of being on the other side of the table, asking for loans, I was now the one with the power to dispense money to promising borrowers.

But my sense of excitement and euphoria quickly dissipated

as the directors' meeting progressed. First of all, they wanted to talk about management matters which I'm sure were important but which didn't interest me in the least.

Then, I really got frustrated when they began to propose and push through big loans on marginal projects that I would never have supported. But I wasn't in this thing alone. I had a board of directors, many of whom certainly knew their business, who had some independent ideas about how to run a bank.

Finally, when the board approved a huge loan for a used car business that I thought would be a losing venture, I decided this field, as important as it was in supporting entrepreneurs, was not for me.

The next day, I contacted some of my business associates and said, "Sell my interest!"

I do a lot of business with banks. But I have discovered over the years that there's a right way and a wrong way to deal with bankers when you're a business person.

Indeed, the approach you take to your banker can determine whether you receive or lose a given loan. So now, how can you get a loan on the best terms possible? Here are several "loan lessons" which you may find helpful as you embark upon your quest for financing.

LOAN LESSON #1: TRY TO GET YOUR LOAN APPROVED BEFORE YOU ALLOW YOUR APPLICATION TO GO THROUGH

Never allow a loan application to go through unless you're 95 percent sure that the loan is going to be approved! It's best never to submit a loan application to a bank if you think it will be turned down because that tends to spoil your banking relations. Also, it's a waste of time and effort, for both you and the bank.

If you get to know your banks, you'll learn what they're looking for and what types of companies they tend to favor. For example, some banks are inclined to lend to manufacturing companies; others go for real estate; and still others are high on high-tech companies. The worst thing you can do is go to a bank with

a project for which they've never before lent money
which they know little or nothing.

So how can you determine which loan applications wi.. ..,
and which won't?

In part it takes some experience with trial and error. You'll
probably have to make a few applications and see them fall flat
before you begin to get the hang of it.

On the other hand, if you do some research beforehand and
get a good lawyer and accountant to guide you and recommend
certain banks and bankers, you'll be much more likely to score
on your first try. This theme of learning to rely on good accountants, lawyers and other professional contacts for loan information
is one which will recur again and again in our discussion of financing.

LOAN LESSON #2: GET A GOOD LOAN OFFICER

If you can find a good loan officer, he should be able to tell you
if your loan application is going to have a good chance of being
approved. An incompetent or inattentive officer may just run your
application through without much thought, have it disapproved
by a committee—and cause you to have a black mark on your
credit record because your loan's been turned down. As you know
if you've ever applied for a loan, there's usually a question on
the application form which goes something like this: "Have you
ever been turned down for a loan?"

A good loan officer can help you avoid this risk, but how do
you find such a person?

The first things you want to look for are savvy and experience.
So it's necessary to chat with your prospective loan officer for a
few minutes to ascertain something about his or her rate of loan
application approval.

After you've described something about your project and
financial background and perhaps shown the officer a business
plan, you might ask: "What are the percentages on my loan application going through?"

Suppose he or she says, "Well, I can't tell you for sure. The
committee will have to make that decision."

In such a case, you'd better get another loan officer or another bank. This person is obviously either lacking in knowledge, or doesn't occupy a very strong position in the bank. Or maybe he's too timid to offer a definite opinion. In either case, he's not the person for you.

On the other hand, suppose the officer says, "Look, I've been in this business fifteen years. In that time, I've only had three loans turned down. My policy is to never take in a loan unless I'm almost certain that it's going to go through."

In this situation, I would feel much more confident. Many young loan officers will take in loan applications either without thinking seriously about their potential or without really understanding how their own bank procedure operates. So I'm much more favorably disposed toward those who indicate they have some special banking savvy about which proposals will fly and which will fail in their bank.

In short, even if you're dealing with a bank for the first time, you should be careful about choosing your loan officer. Certainly, if you're inexperienced as an entrepreneur, you'll lack some of the leverage that you may have in later years, after you've established yourself as a success. But you can still shop intelligently for a sympathetic, understanding loan officer.

At the very least, you should expect your loan officer to give you some assurance that your loan application will be accepted. If you can't get that assurance, you'd be out of your mind to stick with that particular loan officer or that bank. Just pick up your papers and walk over to another bank. Banks are like any other organization that deals with consumers. Some are sensitive to the needs of customers and some are not. If you're a beginner, you need one that's going to be sensitive to your type of loan, and that may mean doing a little leg work to find the right person in the right bank.

Also, don't get discouraged if you get rejected a couple of times. *Everybody* gets turned down at some point, and it really doesn't matter how experienced you are.

One of my proposals may be turned down by two banks, but that doesn't mean I should throw in the towel and forget the project. The rejections can be simply signals that say, "Go back to the drawing board!" You have to figure out if the problem is something you are doing wrong or just the fact that you've gone to the wrong banking institutions.

As it often turns out, there is a problem in the presentation to the banks. Financial experts can straighten out the difficulty, and the next time you may get the loan immediately.

So you need to be prepared for some rejections—and also sometimes for a little arrogance or unpleasantness on the part of the banker. At this stage of my operations, I usually assign one of our accounting or financial experts to deal directly with the bank officers. They then wade through the often slow and difficult process of getting the loan through.

But many entrepreneurs, even those who have been operating for many years, prefer to deal personally with their bankers. And certainly, when you first start out, you'll have to handle the banking and loan applications yourself, with advice from your lawyer and accountant. In any case, it's best to understand the principles involved in getting through to various bankers and bank bureaucracies.

LOAN LESSON #3: ASK YOUR BANKER FOR ADVICE

Bankers, as we've seen, are human beings just like the rest of us. That means that they may be flattered and encouraged if an entrepreneur says, "Hey, I really don't understand such-and-such an aspect of financing a venture. Can you explain to me how it works?"

Most big banks have venture capital departments or similar sections which specialize in start-up enterprises. Most likely, you'll be referred to a bank officer who has some experience in this area if you're just starting an enterprise. And you can get some great advice from these departments if you just go in with the right questions and your ears open.

One large American bank was famous at one time for making small business loans and giving astute advice to fledgling operators who were just starting off in their businesses. But then, they became the "big business bank," and some of the advantages that they had to offer to entrepreneurs disappeared. But there are still plenty of entrepreneur-oriented banks around. So don't hesitate to ask your banker for advice. You may be pleasantly surprised at how much help you can get just by communicating to the officer something about the needs of your new business.

LOAN LESSON #4: LEARN HOW
YOUR BANKER THINKS

Bankers, because of their training and also often because of their peculiar personalities, may seem to think somewhat differently from the rest of us. They're often regarded as a kind of high priesthood of money management, and an aura of mystery may surround their deliberations and decision making.

But after you've dealt with bankers awhile, you begin to comprehend better some of the subtleties of "bank think." As you begin to tune in to their minds, you soon realize they're influenced by common sense as much as the rest of us.

So how exactly *do* bankers think? Here are a few illustrations.

No banker ever wants to make a loan that his bank will have to go to court to collect. If there's even a chance you won't make your payments, they'll be reluctant to deal with you. Underlying this attitude is the legitimate position that all bankers take that they're looking after their stockholders' and depositors' money. If it seems likely that a loan is going to be a trouble loan, which they might have to call in or foreclose upon, they don't want anything to do with it.

Try looking at your company through your banker's eyes, and attempt to identify your strengths and weaknesses. You might ask yourself, "Does it appear quite likely to outsiders that I'm going to be able to repay that loan?" That's the question the banker will ask, and it's the question you have to ask as well.

Suppose, for example, you're in this situation: You're asking for a large amount of money; you're launching an extremely high-risk venture; and you refuse to endorse the loan personally (or even if you're willing to endorse, you have no personal assets to speak of). Under such circumstances, you would definitely be a high-risk client—and you can bet your bank will want to avoid the headaches you're likely going to cause them.

The bigger your loan, the more likely your bank is to regard you as a "partner" rather than a small customer.

Even if you're a new entrepreneur, a bank may be sufficiently impressed to lend you a significant amount of money—say well up into six figures—*if* you have impressive credentials, a great idea and a good staff to back you up. But when a bank decides to go out on a limb for a customer with a loan, that changes the usual shape of "bank think." Specifically, when there's a great deal of money involved, a bank may have no choice but to try to work out a repayment plan if you should get into trouble in your repayment schedule.

In other words, it's much easier for a bank to put the squeeze on a small debtor than it is to take a chance that they'll lose a large amount of money by unsuccessfully trying to call in a large loan. So, if you owe them a million dollars or more and they throw you into bankruptcy, they're the losers as much as you are.

It costs banks a fortune to take loans back. If they foreclose on a loan, they'll often have a 50 percent loss, including their legal fees and other expenses. So it's in their interest, as well as yours, for you to turn your company around. A smart, sympathetic banker will even be willing to help you, both with good advice and maybe with additional loan money—if you can make a persuasive argument that success is just around the corner.

Of course, no one is suggesting that you should try to get an extremely large loan from a bank if you have serious doubts about the viability of your own proposal. These are just some ideas about how bankers are likely to think after they've made a loan and you've unexpectedly gotten into trouble.

At lower amounts, say as far down as the $50,000 to $100,000 range, the bank may threaten to call in a loan more often than they'll actually act to collect. Your key tactic, if you happen to get into this predicament, is to *stay in touch* with them.

If you don't answer their collection notices or other correspondence, you can expect the worst. But if you immediately get on the telephone with your banker when a problem arises, you'll often find there's an attitude of "let's see if we can work this thing out." Certainly, you may run into one of those "killer" banks that are totally ruthless and cold-blooded in a tight money market. But you may just as easily encounter a sympathetic bank officer who's willing to give you a little latitude and assistance in getting your affairs in order.

As we've seen, bankers are human beings just like anybody else. They may have a special kind of "banker's mind." Sometimes, their extensive experience with bad loans may have made them too cautious. At the same time, when an entrepreneur develops a friendship or at least a cordial business relationship, the banker will usually respond accordingly.

LOAN LESSON #5: IDENTIFY AND AVOID THE "KILLER BANKS"

Each bank has its own personality and its own set of moral standards. Some will do everything they can to make a small, new venture succeed. Others are simply interested in getting as much money as they can out of new entrepreneurs. When they get a chance, they'll squeeze and squeeze the life right out of your pet project.

So there are a number of banks that we simply won't borrow from—even though they've made tremendous loan offers to us. We know enough about them to understand that when there's a tight economy, they'll pull their loans back on some pretext and then press unmercifully for the balance owed. They're a disgrace to the American banking system; but they'll probably always be with us, so it's important to learn how they operate and how to avoid them.

Generally speaking, when you go in to make out a loan application, everything is in favor of the bank. There's an old story about a banker who put a stack of papers about three inches high in front of a client who was seeking a loan. The banker said, "Here, read these."

The loan applicant, looking bewildered, said, "Read *all* of these?"

"That's right."

The applicant thought for a moment and then asked, "Tell me, if I don't like something in there and decide not to go along with that section, what happens, do I get the money?"

"No," the banker replied.

"Well," the applicant said, "just show me the last page where I'm supposed to sign."

That's an apocryphal story, but it happens over and over again in real life. In most cases, if you're a "little guy" and you don't sign what they want you to sign, you don't have a prayer of getting your money. And in that sheaf of loan application papers, you can be sure that there are many escape clauses which will allow the bank to recall your loan almost at will.

Of course, many banks are aboveboard and highly ethical in their dealings with business people. They want to see new businesses appear and prosper in their community because they know in the long run a booming business environment will benefit the banking industry as well.

But others are looking mainly for the quick buck. They're willing to make loans they usually would not make in a tight money market.

If the economy is characterized by a "loose" money market, where there's a surplus of funds among lenders, it's usually fairly easy to get a loan from any bank. But when the situation changes, with money becoming tighter and interest rates going up, the "killers," who have been lying in wait for the unwary, begin to stalk their prey.

Certain of these bankers may begin to look over their portfolios and decide that they have too many small, shaky enterprises which are paying low rates for their money. Unable to abide this low-profit state of affairs, they start ripping through the businesses on their lists, pulling in the loans. Then, they'll lend the money out again to customers with triple-A credit ratings.

I had a problem like this myself one time. I had taken out a loan with one bank at a fairly good rate of interest, and I liked the people I was working with.

But then another banker—a real salesman—approached me and convinced me to move my loan to his bank at a much cheaper interest rate. Also, he was offering what seemed to me much easier terms. So I took the bait, and for a while, I was patting myself on the back, thinking I'd make an extremely shrewd decision.

But then we hit a downturn in the economy, and the money

market got quite tight. At this stage in my career, I didn't know about the different personalities of different banks, and the tendency some banks have to become "killers" with customers. But I found out fast enough.

My new banker decided to upgrade his loans, and at the time I wasn't what he regarded as a top-flight loan risk. So he called in my loan, and that put me in a very difficult situation. My business was highly leveraged—that is, we had gone deeply into debt in order to get capital for expansion. This problem with our loan endangered our very existence.

So I did the only thing I really could do. I walked over to my first bank, went right in to the president's office and confessed, "I made a big mistake."

He asked me what had happened, and I told him the trouble I had gotten into with his sharp-dealing colleague across the street. Then, this banker did something that I've never heard of before or since. He wrote me a check for the amount of money I owed and said, "Here, go pay the loan off and bring the account back here to us."

I did just that, and I've never stopped banking with this particular bank. In fact, it's the greatest bank I've ever done business with. The president and his staff understand better than most what it takes to establish and build a healthy, mutually profitable banker-client relationship."

But how can you find out which banks are "killers" and protect yourself from them?

The first step is to ask around. Check with other businesses in your community and see what sort of experience they've had with their banks. It won't take long to uncover the horror stories and also to get some recommendations for the most ethical and professional bank officers.

Finally, don't forget your accountant and lawyer. If they work in the community where you're seeking loans, that's an added advantage. They'll be aware of complaints, lawsuits or just feelings of disaffection with various banks and bankers. Also, they'll be likely to know which are the "killers" and which are the real creators and life-givers for new businesses in the community.

LOAN LESSON #6: TRY TO AVOID GIVING YOUR PERSONAL GUARANTEE FOR LOANS

If you've had any experience at all trying to get loans from banks, this bit of advice may make you think that I've just arrived in the real world from never-never-land. One of the first things that any bank tries to force you to do is to give your personal endorsement to a loan you want. Also, they'll frequently ask for your spouse's signature as well.

The reason for this is obvious: If you sign only in the name of your corporation, and that corporation is a new entity with little or no assets, the bank may never be able to get its money back if you fail to make your payments. Your corporation will limit your liability; but your bank will prefer to lock you up with open-ended obligations.

So they'll insist you sign personally for the loan, and that will allow them to come after you personally—and your spouse as well if she or he has signed on the dotted line. In other words, one wrong move and your entire estate may be wiped out when a killer bank is on one of its search-and-destroy missions.

The word *destroy* isn't too strong in this connection, either. I watched one of the big banks in New York destroy an entrepreneur who thought it could never happen to him. He was working on a deal that seemed so certain to succeed that he became absolutely sure nothing could go wrong. He not only signed for a loan—he also got his wife to give her signature as well.

That was the beginning of his end. His business, a real-estate-related venture, required him to get a building permit (which he had secured) and then to construct a multi-storied building in a residential area. Unexpectedly, however, representatives of the local community filed a lawsuit to stop the construction, and as a result, the forward movement of the enterprise was delayed until the legal hassles could be straightened out. He began to run into cash-flow problems, and soon was technically in default on his loans.

Unfortunately, the entrepreneur had never gotten along too well with one of the loan officers in his bank. So this banker decided to go after him when the legal issues arose. Before the builder realized what had hit him, the bank had broken him and thrown him into bankruptcy. Also, the killer banker put the word out to colleagues at other institutions in the area and encouraged them to pull the entrepreneur's lines of credit.

Although the property which the man had bought was quite valuable and would eventually have allowed him to pay off his debts with full interest, he was never given a chance. Finally—and most tragically—because he and his wife had both signed on the dotted line, his personal holdings were jeopardized along with his business interests.

When you're just starting out, of course, it's necessary to make compromises; and that may include giving your personal endorsement to loans. When I was a beginner, I sometimes signed personally myself. Certainly, there was a risk involved; if anything went wrong, I could have lost everything. But on occasion, if you want to win big, you have to borrow big—and banks are simply not going to shoulder all your risks for you.

As a matter of fact, I've had to go *beyond* the simple personal endorsement to get some banks to back me up. One time, I even went to the famous Lloyd's of London to get them, in effect, to insure my word of honor!

At the time, I was running the Avis Airlines Rent-A-Car company, and the bank we were dealing with would periodically send out auditors to check out the number of cars we owned. The cars were necessary, of course, as collateral to back up the loans we took out to finance the venture.

Unfortunately, however, the cars were often out on the road, and the bank needed some solid assurance that we really owned the number of cars that we said we owned. I sympathized with the bank, because even though they trusted me, they had to answer to the federal authorities for the loans they had on the books. In short, I couldn't get the loans unless federal auditors came in and checked out all our cars.

That's when I came up with my Lloyd's of London idea. I figured that since the famous insurer was willing to protect the legs of Marlene Dietrich, various parts of the anatomy of other actors and actresses, and other odd and assorted items, they should certainly be able to back my word.

So I went to them and proposed that they give me an insurance policy which would guarantee that whatever I signed was true. Lloyd's agreed, the banks were satisfied, and we saved more in auditing fees and other expenses than we paid out in premiums for the insurance!

Of course, this is not to suggest that you should have to go to Lloyd's of London to get your word insured. But you almost have to sign personally in order to qualify for certain loans.

Often, if your personal assets are small, you may not seem to have that much to lose. But still, be careful! If you have to sign personally, be sure that the amount of the loan you're taking out is not so great that it will totally wipe you out and seriously hurt your family. Also, if you can avoid it, *never* allow your spouse to sign with you. Generally speaking, as long as your spouse doesn't sign, assets which are in his or her name can't be touched by any lender that is coming after you for a loan violation.

As you get farther along in your career, however, I would advise you to refuse to endorse anything personally. At least, that's the approach I take. If a deal won't stand on its own, with the cash I'm willing to put in, I don't want anything to do with it.

LOAN LESSON #7: ESTABLISH ACCOUNTS IN SEVERAL BANKS

If you have all your money or all your loans with one bank, that bank can "squeeze" you. In other words, in a tight money market, they may decide to recall your loan or put pressure on you to pay it off in a way you weren't counting on. But if you have loans with two, three or more banks, you don't have as much to worry about.

The safety of having your loan money spread around in several banks is similar to the safety you get with diversification in your investments. It's a basic principle of money management that you should never put all your financial eggs in one basket. The same principle applies when you're taking out business loans.

I've operated on this principle for many years. I simply refuse to put myself in a position where a bank will be able to put the squeeze on any of my operations.

Any bank we deal with could call me up tomorrow and say, "We want our money now!" But because my banking relationships are spread out, I could easily give any single institution their money on demand and not be hurt a bit. But of course, we would never bank with them again. We'd just move all our loans and deposits out permanently and tell that banker to go jump in the lake.

If you're just starting out and are quite limited in your funds, it may not be worthwhile initially to go to more than one bank. But as soon as your finances permit, branch out and begin to deal with several different banking institutions. That way, you'll be safe from the squeeze that any "killer" bank may threaten you with. Also, you'll be protected from other, good banks that may be facing a genuine crisis and feel they must protect their depositors' money.

Finally, a word of caution: Some entrepreneurs who need money but can't convince a bank officer to go along with them may head for one of the storefront finance companies.

This is dangerous business. Generally speaking, finance companies know that people are coming to them because they couldn't get loans through a bank. As a result, the finance operation will typically charge higher interest, and demand much tougher terms. That's when they start asking for your house, your cars, everything you own. You must be prepared to lose all if things go wrong, as they often do.

So stick to the more civilized approaches to getting money for your entrepreneurial idea—such as banks or venture capitalists—and your family will be much happier and safer!

Now, let's assume you've got your money in hand, and you're ready to turn your idea into a multimillion-dollar success. What can you expect along the way?

First of all, as your company grows by leaps and bounds, you'll find yourself crossing what I call the "border into the big time." And like the gunslingers of old, as you cross that border you'll find yourself confronting new challenges which are sure to test your mettle.

Nine

How to Cross the Border Into the Big Time

Or, Why the First Million Is Always the Hardest

*"Few rich men own their own property.
The property owns them."*

*—Robert Green Ingersoll,
"Address to the McKinley League,"
New York, October 29, 1896*

*E*very ambitious entrepreneur has visions of becoming a *super* success.

That may mean an aspiration to be recognized as a business genius . . . to build a sprawling industrial empire . . . to create a product no one has ever dreamed of before . . . to open a market that never existed—or simply to become filthy rich.

What about your entrepreneurial fantasy?

Whatever it is, I'm sure that you don't want to keep your high-flying ambitions in your head or on a drawing board. You want to get out in the real world and drive upward, to the top of some seemingly impossible industrial peak. As far as you're concerned, the sky's the limit with your new venture. Otherwise, you wouldn't be bothering to pull together the financing and management team that you need to make it go.

But the way to the top is by no means an open road, completely free of obstacles. There are difficult borders to cross, especially as you move into the gross revenue range of $500,000 to $1 million. In fact, the $500,000 to $1 million "border" marks a transition phase that has broken many entrepreneurs.

Usually, the beginning entrepreneur gets used to spending his money in a certain idiosyncratic way, in the beginning phase of his venture. He'll make a profit despite the fact that he does much of the management work himself (i.e., he "wears four or five hats") and he neglects using industry norms of cost that become quite important beyond the million-dollar mark. But then, if he's successful in making his enterprise grow, he begins to run into overhead expenses that he'd never anticipated. It's rather ironic. His entire future may be threatened by the magnitude of his early success.

The additional costs that he encounters begin to whip and lash him from a variety of directions. He finds he needs more space, so his rent goes up. He needs a larger staff to meet the increasing demand, so his employee costs begin to soar. At the start, he did all the selling. But as broader markets beckon, he pours more and more money into advertising—and these promotion costs rapidly threaten to career out of control.

Then, there's the government. After you set up a corporation and begin to bring on extra personnel, you have to provide pensions, medical insurance and other fringe benefits. These, along with the tax withholding and other requirements from the Internal Revenue Service, cause your federal, state and local paperwork to begin piling up.

When most entrepreneurs enter this rough transition phase, they usually find that they have a great deal to learn. The one-man show mentality leads to serious crises as the industry norms for cost become reality. During this phase, profits may actually drop to zero. Certainly, there's a lot of pride that an entrepreneur may feel in topping the $1 million mark in gross revenues. But once the feelings of pride have run their course, the more abiding emotion can be summed up like this:

"I'm just working for other people! What's the point in building up this business if all I'm doing is paying out money, right and left, to other people?"

Even though an entrepreneur may be grossing $1 million, he may not be paying himself any more than when he was at a half million or less. Why? In part, the additional revenues are eaten up by extra administrative costs. This is one reason business pundits often say, "The first million is always the hardest." The transition from about a half million to a million in gross revenues seems particularly rough because of the lack of extra compensation enjoyed by the entrepreneur.

Some have even suggested that it's reasonable for many entrepreneurs to remain rather small. If you can gross $300,000 or $400,000 annually, pay yourself a hefty salary and avoid the administrative headaches of size that accompany the million-dollar mark, why push yourself?

That may be a reasonable argument on its face, but it won't convince the hard-driving types. In most cases, they've launched the business with the idea of seeing just how far they can take it. Frankly, any argument about limiting growth in order to avoid management headaches just wouldn't register. Their attitude is simple and straightforward: "Who wants to stay small?" they ask. "I don't want a Mom-and-Pop store—I want the world!"

And I must say, I agree with this mentality myself. Sure, there are going to be hassles and headaches as you grow. But Hannibal's Elephant Show didn't make it across the Alps without some slips, bumps and losses. And the California gold rush crowd didn't set up stakes outside Sacramento just to pan enough nuggets to supply a small town jewelry shop. They had their eyes fixed on massive riches—and that's the level of ambition harbored by most entrepreneurs.

If your own ambitions tend to run to outrageous heights, then it's likely you'll run smack into the barrier that plagues other business gunslingers who begin to experience significant success. You'll find you're being held back because of the obstacles to growth that lurk at the $500,000 to $1 million level of gross revenues.

So what can you do to prepare for the challenges that will occur at this "border to the big time"? Simply this: Learn what the key hurdles are, and begin right now to get your company in shape to sail over them. Also, remember that industry cost norms will be close to your own costs, so follow them! A loss of 1 percent in any phase of your operations is 1 percent—and a few percentage points can mean the difference between profit and loss.

There are a myriad of management and personnel problems that arise as you get larger. You have to hire more people, and you also have to learn to delegate authority. As you move toward the million-dollar mark, you'll find you can no longer wear five or six "hats" in running the business; you'll have to cut your "hands-on" involvement in daily operations back to only two or three of those "hats."

We'll be dealing with many of these management and personnel problems elsewhere in the book. For now, let's concentrate on those issues during the transition that are most closely tied to dollars-and-cents considerations.

There are some good features and some bad ones that occur during expansion; this is true for everyone. The challenge is to minimize the negatives and accentuate the positives. To this end, you should anticipate three hurdles that are likely to inflate your overhead-related costs to the danger point—your work force, your office space and your paperwork.

THE STAFFING HURDLE

Such questions as when you're going to bring extra people into your company to help you, and how much you're going to pay them, present some of the trickiest issues any business person has to face. Clearly, as the volume of your business increases, you're going to have to bring on extra secretarial and clerical workers; and when you do, you'll have to pay them at the going rate.

Also, you'll find that any helpers who may have assisted you in getting off the ground will want to be paid wages equal to those of the newcomers. In other words, you may get your sister-in-law to work for you for a month or two or even longer when you're just starting. But once that little honeymoon is over and you start to make enough money to bring on extra people, she'll want to be paid just like everybody else.

There's another side to this coin as well. Some inexperienced entrepreneurs feel so grateful for their early success that they may be tempted to give away more than they're making to some of their old employees.

After beginning to take in a little money, one company that we invested in started throwing around raises to everyone in sight. And I mean *enormous* raises. They actually seemed to believe the old saw that money grows on trees—at least that's what I concluded as they raised secretarial salaries from $12,000 to $20,000 a year and hiked lower-management people by 30 percent or more.

All this was done without sufficient prior planning, and predictably, the company began to run into a serious cash flow problem. But fortunately, in our role as venture capitalists, we had retained some influence over the management. So our people were able to intervene and get this company back on the right track with their salary and expense account policies.

This isn't by any means an isolated example, either. In another company—a small health services outfit that provided a complete testing program for heart patients—the revenue started coming in at an incredible rate. In the first couple of years, the company's earnings leaped 300 to 400 percent, and the euphoric president suddenly decided that he was going to reward everybody on the premises with prince's wages.

First, he raised the salaries of treadmill technicians from a range of $15,000 to $18,000, up to a range of $30,000 to $35,000. Moreover, employees on every level were given pay hikes of 100 percent or more.

Then, the inevitable happened. Other entrepreneurs in the area saw the profit potential in the cardiac-testing area, and they soon set up shop themselves. And the increased competition caused the first entrepreneur's revenues to plummet.

Before long, he found himself in the sticky situation of having to release some employees and roll back the wages of others. Staff morale in the company hit rock bottom, and this man never achieved the promise of great success that had seemed to be his for the asking. Clearly, he did his employees and himself a disservice.

During the transition phase from a smaller to a big-time business you're likely to confront even more subtle staffing problems than these. Generally speaking, as you get larger, the *percentage* of costs required to produce and sell your product will remain about the same. For example, the bigger you get, the more typing will have to be done. And that will mean hiring more secretaries at the going salary rate. Also, as you broaden your market and sell more of your goods, you'll have to add more salespeople. But in both instances, as volume keeps rising, your employee costs will probably remain a relatively fixed percentage of your gross revenues.

The hiring issue gets trickier as you're confronted with such questions as: "Should I bring on an extra employee right now? Or should I wait a few weeks or months until my sales potential increases even more?"

Obviously, if you act too soon, your new employees won't be able to pull their own weight, and profits will drop. Unless they can generate enough business to cover their own compensation and other costs, they won't be much immediate help in your efforts to grow faster. In any case, you can't expect miracles to happen with new employees overnight. They will always cost extra money when they're getting started.

On the other hand, if you wait too long to beef up your staff, competitors may step in and snap up your opportunities. Excessive caution can undercut your potential as easily as foolhardy risk-taking.

I'm reminded of the situation confronted by two attorneys who were taking in about $400,000 a year, with 50 percent of that gross revenue going into running the office. In this case, each lawyer was able to take home about $100,000 a year.

But they sensed that there was a potential for them to provide even more legal services. So they brought an associate onto the staff at $50,000.

The problem was that there was more to the matter than just paying the extra guy $50,000 and then watching the profits go up. Instead, the two senior attorneys quickly realized that it was going to take a few months for the new lawyer to get settled and begin to pull his weight. In the meantime, they were paying him at the rate of $50,000, and the overhead required to support him went up proportionately. In other words, they had to pay the new man his $50,000 salary out of their own compensation, *and* come up with another $50,000 in secretarial costs and other expenses for him.

The bottom line was that the new lawyer had to start bringing in *at least* $100,000 worth of business *fast*. Otherwise, the two senior partners were going to have to reduce their own incomes and drastically cut back on their life-styles. In this case, the new lawyer didn't bring in enough extra business, and the senior attorneys had to make up the difference out of their own pay. One wanted to keep the new man on; the other wanted to let him go. As a result, relationships in the office became strained, and the partnership eventually broke up.

This is a simple but typical illustration of the kind of challenge every entrepreneur must face as he or she moves into the half-million to million-dollar transition. Crisis after crisis hits in the staffing area because there's almost always a temporary squeeze on cash flow as the new people come on board. The first few months that a person spends on a job are almost always the most unproductive. While the newcomer is learning the ropes and making mistakes, the owner has to take up the slack.

But unfortunately, just a few unproductive people in a small operation can break the business. If that new secretary, salesperson or attorney is still spinning his or her wheels after six months or a year and is failing to help generate income, the entire business may well begin to falter.

That's the difference between a small and large company—and it's also one reason why this painful transition phase is so important. There will almost always be far fewer employees when your business is in the half-million-dollar gross revenue range than when you're pulling in millions. As a result, the failure of a few employees to produce will be magnified—and may mean the difference between success and failure. In contrast, a larger company can make do with unproductive people for a while, so long as there are enough productive members of the staff to counter the negative effects.

Take the typical sales organization. We know that if we hire one additional salesperson to open a new branch and set him up properly until it begins to pay off, that will cost us at least $150,000. This calculation includes the costs of setting up an office; giving the person backup clerical systems; paying his salary for a year; maintaining expense accounts; and other such sales-related outlays.

If the salesperson becomes productive after a few months, then it's all been worth it. But if he's the type who is inefficient, inexperienced or lazy—and especially if he leaves before the year is out—we may lose much of the $150,000 that was spent to get him started. In fact, even if the person is successful, it will still take two or three years to get our investment back.

So there's always a risk. If the new employee doesn't work out, the entire business will suffer. On the other hand, if he does work out, he could play a key role in helping you to push beyond that $1 million mark, into the big time.

THE SPACE HURDLE

Many businesses these days have been launched in an entrepreneur's garage or apartment—especially in fields that don't require a great deal of space to house inventories. For example, a number of people operating in limited physical facilities have become quite wealthy and successful in high-tech industries, such as the production of computer software.

But as your revenues start moving well up into the six-figure range, you'll find you simply can't operate out of a telephone booth. You'll have to rent an office; and before long you'll probably have to rent still *another* office to house your growing staff. Also, you'll probably need increasing amounts of factory and warehouse space.

During this transition phase, there are several factors to keep in mind as far as space is concerned. The first is that expenses related to your business space—your rent, light, heat and other such outlays—tend to be fixed. That is, they stay about the same, even if your revenues are increasing.

So, suppose your volume goes up from $1 million to $2 million. You may need more salespeople and a larger secretarial staff, and you'll certainly have to spend more money in producing additional products.

But if you can squeeze in more people, you may *not* need any more space. Consequently, as your gross sales and revenues go up, the percentage of your expenses attributable to your office space will decline—and you'll become more profitable.

One illustration of how this works involved a company which was in the midst of this transition phase that we've been talking about. They were doing about $1 million in gross revenues, and they were paying rent equal to about 4 percent of those gross revenues.

Now, that much rent is high: Rent should usually be limited to less than 2 percent of gross revenues. But sometimes, when you're just starting out in a relatively high-rent area, you have to pay a higher percentage for your space than you might like.

In any case, this company soon shot up to $2 million in gross sales, but they found that they didn't need to rent any more space to produce that volume of business. As a result, their percentage of rent dropped to 2 percent, or a more acceptable amount than they were paying at one million. This company had taken a gamble on extra space, and it paid off.

To make this crystal-clear, it may be helpful to lay the specific calculations out in detail: At $1 million in revenues, they were paying 4 percent of their gross revenues, or $40,000. And since they didn't have to rent additional space, their rent remained fixed at $40,000. Thus when their revenues increased to $2 million, the percentage of rent that they were paying declined to 2 percent—or $40,000/$2 million.

What can we learn from this example?

First of all, when your business begins to burgeon in that transition phase, you'll probably find you have to move from your home or small office to a larger space. At this point, you may decide to take *more* space than you immediately need.

If you can afford it, this may be a wise decision, just to allow for a future increase in the volume of your business. But if you do take more space than you need, you may be paying a relatively large proportion of your gross revenues in rent during the transition phase. This is a point where it's wise to be cautious. Rent payments can make the difference between profit and loss. If a few other factors in your business, such as management or staffing, are also out of control, a high rent can quickly spell *disaster*—with a capital *D*! It can become the "extra bucket that sank the boat"!

Even if everything else is in balance, expensive space may put a serious squeeze on your cash flow. That's one of the reasons that it may seem, in the half-million to million-dollar revenue range, that you're "working for others." There just doesn't seem to be enough money to go around because you're paying not only for your current business, but also for business that you expect to be generating in the near future.

Still, if you've chosen your space wisely during this phase and you continue to grow, you'll be thankful that you have some room to expand. And as your revenue goes up and your fixed costs, such as rent, stay the same, you'll find that your profits will increase. So, in the example that we've just considered, when the percentage of rent went down by 2 percent, the percentage of profit went *up* by 2 percent.

Of course, there's always some risk. If business increases, you may be proven smart in your choice of space. If business decreases, you may be broke. So don't bet too heavily on future profits and sales when you're deciding on current rent.

A corollary to all this rent business is that even as you're anticipating future revenue increases, you've got to be very wise and shrewd about choosing the best, most economical space for your company. Some entrepreneurs want too much high-class office status too soon. They think, "It's important to impress my clients. I've simply got to get an office in a blue-blooded district."

But that kind of thinking can put you out of business before you even get started. Again, it's all a matter of percentages. Suppose you spend 10 percent of your revenues on a classy, "uptown" office space when you could be spending only 2 percent. That means you've lost 8 percent out of your ultimate profit margin at the outset—or the kind of money which may well be the difference between profit and loss, success and failure.

Many publishers in Manhattan have learned this lesson the hard way; and increasing numbers are moving to lower-rent districts so that they can beef up their profit margins. They've had offices for years in the midtown and Upper East Side areas in Manhattan, which demand some of the highest rents in the country. And these high costs for office space have played a part in forcing a number of publishers out of business.

In recent years, however, a number of publishers have moved into the downtown areas which have much lower rents. They've found that they simply can't compete in high rent areas—in fact they can't even stay in business, in some cases—unless they cut costs. And the logical place in a high-rent area like Manhattan is to reduce what you spend for office space.

So it pays to give some extremely careful thought to *where* you should set up shop for your enterprise. To clear the office space hurdle, you first have to choose a space that is going to be cheap enough to keep your cashflow and profits up as high as possible. At the same time, the space should be large enough and additional space should be available to accommodate future growth (if you're convinced growth will actually occur).

Finally, you must weigh carefully just how luxurious or high-class your offices really have to be. If you're absolutely *sure* that snooty status is an essential ingredient to your success—and it usually is not—then you may have to pay more money than someone in another type of business. But in most cases, business people can get along on a lot less status than they think they can. The entrepreneur who takes out a lease on the Rolls-Royce office—and uses real Rolls-Royces for limousines—may make a flashy burst on the entrepreneurial firmament. But more often than not, when business turns down—and it *will* turn down—he then disappears without a trace.

THE PAPERWORK HURDLE

As you move toward the million-dollar mark in gross revenues, one of the most unsettling things you'll probably encounter will be a veritable blizzard of paperwork.

When your business is smaller, you tend to ignore many administrative matters—or at least, you put them off and do them in bunches some evening. Your tax notices and your bills accumulate. Finally, to avoid penalties or shutdown of services, you respond in a flash and set everything straight, at least until the next brief crisis a couple of months in the future.

You may get away with this rather slipshod administrative approach when your business is still below about a $400,000 yearly gross. But things start getting more serious when you pass the half-million to million-dollar "border."

At that point, you take on new employees and increase the size of your operation; also, your paperwork multiplies at a geometric rate. As was mentioned at the beginning of this chapter, you have to deal with increasing red tape related to unemployment compensation, health insurance, withholding taxes and various other governmental requirements. Also, the sheer volume of administrative responsibilities involving billpaying, ledgerkeeping and other such matters can drive any normal person nearly crazy. Any new business without experienced staff in these fields will face some rough sledding.

Some entrepreneurs try to handle this increase in administrative volume all by themselves; but they quickly find that they're doing almost nothing but administration. There are not enough hours in the day for them to do all the paperwork and also the thinking and acting necessary to generate new business. Red tape can indeed strangle the growth of a business if an entrepreneur doesn't develop adequate management systems to deal with growth during this transition phase.

To some extent, the paperwork problem can be alleviated by hiring additional staff, such as bookkeepers and clerial workers. But before long, you'll have to start bringing in a computer—and this can be either your salvation or your swan song, depending on how you handle it.

Of course, some entrepreneurs get into the world of computers while they're still quite small. One businessman paid about $3,000 for a small personal computer and then purchased another $7,000 in computer software and accessories. He even went down to a local computer school for a half-day course to try to learn how to work this machine that he had bought.

Now, I would estimate that this man's time is worth about $500 a day. He grosses about a half-million dollars a year, and much of that income has to be attributed to his personal contacts and energies.

Now, think about this situation for a moment: It really makes a lot of sense, doesn't it, for a $500-a-day executive to run down and take a half-baked course in elementary key punching?

I told him he was crazy to take this approach, but he went ahead anyhow. Soon, he found himself spending more time trying to operate the computer than he had been devoting to administrative responsibilities and paperwork *without* the computer!

So he came back and said, "Okay, suppose I hire somebody to run the computer. I've been looking around, and I can see it's going to cost me $20,000 a year or more for the person's salary. Is that really going to be worth it?"

He also had a myriad of other questions: What if his computer disks were damaged and he lost crucial office files? he wondered. Also, as his business expanded, how should he go about adding additional office stations and terminals?

Obviously, the man didn't have the first notion about how to computerize his office. Yet he had tried to do the entire job himself, and he was on the verge of making a mess of it—not to mention the huge amount of money he was in danger of losing. You can spend $100,000 before you even turn around when you get involved with computers.

Fortunately, this entrepreneur found out that he was on the

wrong track before he had made more than a minimal investment of his time and money. He learned that the only way to do a job the right way is to shop around for a top-notch computer consulting firm to help him enter the computer age in the best, most inexpensive way.

If you go about this task haphazardly, you'll pay a huge price sooner than later. But if you approach the issue intelligently and systematically, with a properly chosen consultant or at least plenty of personal research, you may well find that the paperwork hurdle isn't a hurdle at all. A properly computerized office, set up in such a way that it can grow along with overall company expansion, can help you cross the half-million to million-dollar border.

These are just three examples of hurdles that confront everyone who hopes to make the transition to a much larger operation. In every case, the name of the game is efficiency. Whether you're dealing with computers, staffing issues, space rentals or anything else, it's absolutely essential that you always keep efficiency upper-most in your mind. As the old saw goes, "Watch the pennies, and you'll make the dollars."

Fast growth is fine and exciting. But there's a big difference between disciplined, productive growth and an uncontrolled entrepreneurial sprawl. Once you start stumbling around in the midst of major growth, it may *appear* that a healthy expansion is under way. But remember: In a business enterprise, just as in the human body, out-of-control cells can grow too rapidly and eventually destroy the entire organism.

This border which separates a small operation from a big-time business may cause some stresses and strains. It can also be extremely nerve-racking because you'll have to learn a lot about business that you never knew before. Finally, you'll have to make a lot of decisions that will be crucial to your future.

But, when all is said and done, gigantic growth is ultimately what entrepreneurial gunslinging is all about. If you want to remain small, that's fine. Plenty of people can be satisfied with a moderately comfortable income from a business they've built from the ground up. But most true entrepreneurs want to take their business concept as far as it will go. That means running, pushing, pulling and even dragging that business onward and upward.

Rousseau was absolutely right when he said, "The first guinea is sometimes more difficult to acquire than the second million." In fact, I'd take that one step further and say that the first million is *always* harder to make than the second.

But once you've passed that million-dollar mark, you'll find that you've entered a new country which has its own special problems—not the least of which is the need to reach out beyond yourself and seek help from a competent management team. It's a frontier territory which will present you with managerial challenges that were mostly hidden from sight while you were still a Mom-and-Pop operation.

Ten

Why Lone Rangers Make Lousy Entrepreneurs

*"Plans fail for lack of counsel,
but with many advisers they succeed."*

—*Proverbs 15:22*
(New International Version)

A popular image of the successful entrepreneur is that of the independent wheeler-dealer who specializes in solitary high-wire acts over the business world. He is a law unto himself—neither wanting nor needing the help of another human being.

In short, the entrepreneur assumes the aura of a kind of "lone ranger" of industry and finance.

But the popular myth doesn't match up too well with hardnosed reality. True, entrepreneurs do tend to have more control over their time, goals and lives than the typical corporate employee. But they don't by any means exist in a vacuum.

In fact, the entrepreneur who tries to operate alone, without the advice, help and support of others, will surely stumble and fail unless he quickly changes his ways. This is one of the major lessons that you, as an ambitious business person, must learn if you hope to succeed in a big way with your own enterprise.

One of the reasons that we've developed this "lone ranger" image of the successful entrepreneur is that America is what's known as a "conflict society." People and interest groups in America are always butting heads. Competitive businesses spar and undercut each other; ambitious individuals map out strategies to outdo opponents; and employees and employers constantly maneuver to gain some advantage. Business fights government and government fights business. Management fights the unions and unions fight management. In short, conflict reigns supreme on every level.

The Japanese, in contrast, have what you might call a "consensus society." They are oriented toward problem solving. Various individuals and interest groups there tend to work together to achieve common goals that will help everyone. Also, whereas Americans stress interaction between managers in building a team, the Japanese emphasize the participation of *all* workers. They are more cooperative in running their businesses and making their decisions. As a result, in many ways the Japanese are more efficient and productive than we are.

Aspiring entrepreneurs would do well to study the Japanese. You see, the best way to build a foundation for big business success is to build a *team*—and to encourage groups of experts and interested individuals to put their heads together to solve problems and make better decisions.

In Japan, it's relatively easy to put together such a management team because the underlying culture supports this concept. In American culture, on the other hand, despite our interest in team sports, the star system tends to be the ideal. Those with even a modicum of talent and ambition want to rise above the crowd. They want to "do their own thing"; exercise some special set of rights; or express some inner, individualistic impulse.

Perhaps the major obstacle to true business teamwork in America is the mentality of our bosses—and that includes plenty of entrepreneurs. Teamwork requires sharing ideas and listening. But the top people in our corporations are basically authoritarian and egomaniacal. As a result, they're not particularly interested in bringing in team-oriented decision making because if they do, they will automatically lose some of their personal power.

In our society, autocratic bosses, acting more or less unilaterally, can torpedo even the best of others' ideas—ideas which could make everyone involved more successful. Let's illustrate with one of my frustrating experiences a few years ago.

Using a form of consensus decision making, we came up with an excellent idea for an airline reservation cancellation system. The concept was developed after painstaking research and in-depth discussions with experts and colleagues from a variety of pertinent fields. The upshot was that I was extremely excited because I was absolutely certain it would work.

The basic purpose of our concept was to fill empty seats and enable airlines to avoid overselling tickets in their effort to fill flights; the specific method was to get seats canceled in time to allow other passengers to fly. As a matter of fact, we had determined the nation's airlines could achieve a savings of approximately $500 million a year if they could put extra travelers on board in empty seats created by the "no shows" at each flight.

Also, overselling causes tremendous inconvenience for travelers, and can give an airline a terrible reputation. Regular flyers get disgusted when they arrive at an airport and find that their reservations on the plane are gone because the flight has been oversold. The refunds, cash payments and other premiums that are handed out can never compensate the busy traveler for the inconvenience and stress caused by overbooking.

Here's the way the system was supposed to work:

A company we planned to set up would handle the cancellation of reservations for all airlines in the country through one 800 number. Speaking to an automatic recording device, the caller would give his name, airline, the date, the flight number and the time of the flight being cancelled. There would be no busy phone lines or waiting. Our computers would then notify the airline involved that one of its reservations had been cancelled. (Of course, the customer could still call the airline directly to cancel if he liked.) According to our research, this recording procedure by itself could have eliminated one-third of the reservations personnel of the nation's airlines!

We even planned to allow cancellations to be recorded up to one hour *after* flight time. This would enable anyone who had been delayed in getting to the airport plenty of time to get to a phone. The reason? We wanted to encourage travelers to get into the *habit* of canceling their reservations.

What about those who failed to cancel? The airlines would notify our company of all "no-shows." We would then send a letter to each "no-show" who had not canceled, reminding the person that he did not fly on such-and-such a flight, even though he had made a reservation. Also, we would tell the passenger he was now liable to pay a relatively small non-cancellation penalty of $3.

Many times, we would expect the passenger to write, "But I *did* cancel the reservation!" In that case, we would just thank the person politely and let the matter drop.

The purpose of this penalty wouldn't be to make money. Rather, we wanted to put moral pressure on people to cancel their flight on the next occasion so that other passengers could fly. We'd also identify and put pressure on passengers who made two or three reservations on different airlines on the same day, without cancelling any of them.

Of course, some people would not be discouraged from "no-showing" by our first letter. Most likely by the second or third time, however, many passengers would say, "Oh the heck with it!" and would mail in the $3.

Once they sent in the cancellation penalty, it should begin to dawn on them that it would be easier and cheaper to spend a quarter to make a call, rather than pay the $3 penalty and have a "no-show" entered against their record.

In any case, our purpose would always remain the same: Get the unused reservations canceled so that another passenger can fly.

As a result of our in-house discussions, we decided that when we had a series of ten to twenty no-shows on the same person, we would report that to the airline. Then, the airline would decide whether to continue to make reservations for chronic no-show passengers.

As we conceived this concept in our team discussions, the basic idea was very similar to that of the parking ticket. As you know, when you start accumulating parking tickets, you become much more careful: The enforcement agency keeps records, and you know that you'll have to go before a judge if you get too many. We decided the same psychological effect could work with airline passengers.

In presenting this proposal to the airlines' presidents and other executives, we emphasized that the $3 charges would cover our costs of running the program. Also, as I've already indicated, the system would save the airlines $500 million annually. We were certain that the approach would make as much sense to them as it did to us.

But the airline executives flatly refused to adopt our system. Why? As I've thought back over their rejection of the concept, I realize that there was a fundamental difference between the way we formulated the idea and the way we presented it to the airlines. And that difference goes right to the heart of consensus decision making.

The decision-making process in our companies has been sufficiently fine-tuned that we can almost always tell whether an idea like this will "fly." But in this case, consensus decision-making techniques weren't employed in communicating the idea to the airlines. Because they didn't think of the idea themselves, or at least help to formulate it, they rejected it as no good.

Airline companies, like most other American business organizations, are conflict-oriented. When an outsider—or any nonmanagement representative—comes in and tries to sell them a concept, their first reaction is negative.

They wonder, "What is this guy trying to put over on me?"

Or they'll think: "This idea didn't come from our offices; so it could make us look bad or inadequate if we accept."

Or perhaps the top executive might worry: "If I accept an idea like this, my people may be unhappy because it came from the outside."

Some airlines executives told us they had already thought of the idea before. In most cases, I suspect their negativism arose from the fact that they *hadn't* thought of it themselves.

It was necessary for most of the airlines to accept the proposal for it to work. It would also have been necessary to get CAB approval of the concept—a hurdle which would not have been difficult to clear. Yet if we had sat down with these executives and worked the idea through with them, we might have gotten the proposal off the ground. In fact, I'm convinced the idea would *still* work and could *still* save the airlines millions of dollars. As they participated with us, the idea would in effect have become theirs as well as ours. In particular, they would have made improvements on ways to implement the concept.

But unfortunately, our business culture is not set up this way. It's difficult or impossible to have a free interchange of ideas between an established corporation and an "outside" entrepreneur. Also, it's rare for a company with a powerful chief executive officer to be open to any sort of ideas from the outside, including a team approach to decision making.

But in a business that has accepted consensus decision making, things are quite different. Everyone has an equal right to speak. You gather all points of view, and then together, you come up with a better solution that everyone can understand and support.

The result is the end of the era when one boss can make an arbitrary, unilateral decision and then order everybody to carry it out. With this I-say-it-you-do-it approach, the employees following orders usually do so half-heartedly, and that attitude doesn't exactly enhance productivity.

In contrast, in an open discussion, employees learn more about how different ideas can work to effect solutions to different problems. As they participate and offer their own contributions, the ideas become their own, and there's more likely to be wholehearted grassroots support.

Of course, this team approach may be hard to swallow for the top guy who thinks he's "smarter than hell." In fact, it may become painfully evident during the group discussions that the boss really isn't as smart as he thinks he is. And some "dummies" may turn out to have great ideas!

Clearly, an emphasis on teamwork and consensus decision making can be threatening to any boss who likes to take ego trips. That's why many macho American business leaders and entrepreneurs, entrapped by a lone ranger mentality, avoid the Japanese system like the plague.

Our culture is a wonderful breeding ground for the independent, gunslinging entrepreneur who can take almost any good business idea and run with it. But when that entrepreneur reaches the half-million to million-dollar transition point in his growing business, the importance of his independence and initiative begins to give way to a demand for management and decision-making skills. It's at this point that many entrepreneurs begin to run into big trouble because they haven't learned to listen and work with others.

But have no fear! There is a way of escape out of this dilemma—a way which has been variously termed "the quality circle" "team management," or just "the way the Japanese do it." And the Japanese aren't the only ones who are sold on this concept.

Through years of research at a behavioral science laboratory in Michigan, we've developed a version of team management and decision making. This approach, a procedure protected by copyright called Shared Participation, can be a powerful antidote to any entrepreneur's lone ranger syndrome. The gunslinger's ego usually remains intact, and more important, the staff members become solidly committed to working together as a team. They work out the solutions to various problems in a process that conceals their identities and subordinates their self-interest to the good of the entire organization.

THE NOT-SO-LONE RANGER

In general, the "Shared Participation" version of consensus decision making includes these key factors:

1. You first identify a specific problem, and your main goal is to solve that problem. Then, you gather together a group of thirty of your people and divide them into six five-person teams to solve this given business problem. Our research has confirmed that five people constitute the perfect size working team for this type of consensus decision making.

2. The thirty members must possess as a group (though not necessarily as individuals) sufficient knowledge of the problem; experience; native intuition; and other skills and abilities that can be used to come up with a proper solution.

3. Each member of each five-person team should fill out an anonymous evaluation sheet, outlining his seven best solutions to the problem. Then, he should reduce his list to the five best solutions. In our Shared Participation sessions, this evaluation is done on a secret ballot that requires each person to evaluate in depth all sides of a problem.

4. Then, the members of each five-person team turn in their evaluation sheets to an individual not involved in the decision-making process. This nonparticipant should scramble them and write down all twenty-five ideas on one master solution sheet. The original ballots should then be destroyed while the team observes, to ensure anonymity.

5. Copies of this master sheet are next passed around to each member of a five-person team; and in an open discussion, they proceed to consolidate duplicate answers and exchange any new ideas. It always becomes evident during this process that five

minds are better than one. Together, they each have five times the knowledge and experience that each does alone.

6. Finally, in their discussion or sharing session, the members of each five-person team strive to reach a consensus over what the five best solutions to the problem should be. Again, our research has shown that it takes no more than five solutions to solve any problem. Moreover, when five people agree on a solution, they all understand and support it and stand ready to work for it in a way they would never do if they merely received orders from on high.

The consensus decision making which occurs in a single five-person team is just the first step. Remember: There will be a total of six five-person teams focusing on the same problem at the same time.

After each five-person team has come up with its own five solutions, the members are so committed to what they've accomplished as a team that they're practically willing to fight anyone who dares to disagree with them!

As you can see, an important psychological transformation is taking place. Five individuals have come into a room, and out of the Shared Participation process they've emerged as a unit. They now have a group identity, instead of five fragmented egos. As a result, they're ready for the next step—to leave behind their small team and become part of an even larger team.

So what happens next is that each five-person team is combined with another five-person team to produce three ten-person teams out of the total participating group of thirty.

But we don't just throw these ten people together and let them begin to tear the guts out of each other! Instead, we seat them around a round table—it wasn't by accident that King Arthur chose this shape—and assign the members of each team to alternate chairs. This way, they are merged together into a new group, so that there's less intense identification with their original team of five.

Then, a nonparticipant in the discussion takes each set of five ideas which the two five-person teams have come up with, scrambles the list and presents them as a list of ten for consideration by the newly formed ten-person team.

As in the initial five-person procedure, the ten-person team will get rid of duplicates and then will begin sharing ideas about how they can reduce the remaining items to five.

When this team of ten has finished its work, their five ideas will be presented with the five ideas each which the other two groups of ten have formulated. In other words, all thirty people are now involved together in the decision-making process.

Usually, a nonparticipant will write all fifteen ideas on a blackboard in full view of all thirty people who have been participating in the process. By this time, everyone is so involved in the Shared Participation approach that they have, in effect, merged into one corporate "brain." No single human brain can do what they are now capable of accomplishing together. Also, the procedure goes much more quickly, because they've become accustomed to the Shared Participation process.

Of course, this type of consensus decision making doesn't have to be limited to thirty people. We usually think in terms of thirty-member groups, but you could just as easily follow the procedure with sixty or ninety people.

This entire process, from setting up the decision-making groups to making a decision or finding the best solution, can be completed in a matter of hours, and usually no more than one working day—provided it's conducted properly.

But let me hasten to say that Shared Participation is *not* just another form of brainstorming. In brainstorming, people usually start off by throwing around ideas in a freewheeling discussion. Usually, however, a few dominant individuals manage, through force of personality, superior logic, or their position of authority to impose their ideas on the others. Some quiet or reserved people never get their point across. Others give up too easily, or they alienate a significant segment of the group so that their views are discounted.

The final result is often put down as a "consensus," even though it's really not that at all. Rather, these brainstorming solutions are merely half-baked, poorly reasoned and partially accepted decisions that may well be worse than what any one individual might have made.

In contrast, the Shared Participation concept is designed to eliminate many human roadblocks, such as egotism and self-vested interest, in solving a problem. If things are kept anonymous in the initial sharing of ideas, many problems stemming from prejudice, an inferiority complex or other personality quirks or deficiencies can be eliminated. Nobody knows who originated what idea, so the personality hurdles connected with any given idea disappear.

Of course, not everybody in one of these decision-making groups will be on the same level in the corporation. Typically, there may be one or two individuals who are higher in the management structure than the others. As a result, some readers may worry about the danger of a boss imposing his will on everybody else.

The bottom line here is that each boss must leave his management authority at the door when he joins in one of these discussions. Also, in most Shared Participation procedures, there will be other five-person teams that the boss is not a member of and thus cannot possibly dominate. The ideas for a solution shouldn't be identified with the boss or any other individual; they must be identified with the group as a whole. This approach will always work toward the greatest good for the organization.

What the boss gains through consensus decision making will far outweigh what he could gain in always trying to force his views on his subordinates. The authoritarian approach will lead at best only to half-hearted support, or at worst to an active wish by the employee for the boss to fail.

Certainly, however, the buck ultimately has to stop with a top manager. Neither you nor any other entrepreneur who has founded a business is going to be willing to let employees in your company run wild with your capital and ideas. As a result, it's always assumed in the Shared Participation process that top-level management will have to make about 10–20 percent of a company's decisions apart from the consensus decision-making procedure. Also, we recommend that as a general rule, the chief executive officer of a company should not participate because his or her presence would be too authoritative for the system to work properly.

But at the same time, it's important to maintain the integrity of the Shared Participation approach if you want to get the maximum mileage out of the expertise of your management team. So, if a person with seniority or special authority is involved in one of these Shared Participation sessions, he should make it clear that he's just "one of the guys." He has one voice, and it's just as important for him to work toward consensus as it is for the others. The way the Shared Participation teams are set up will facilitate his involvement.

During the discussions you must emphasize *honesty* in critiquing ideas and the value of fair discussion in working for the ultimate goals of the organization. Moreover, you must limit your own executive power for a period of time so that you don't in any way suggest that you're trying to impose a solution on the others. The objective is to elicit all feasible ideas that will lead to the best possible answer.

Some other points to keep in mind during the Shared Participation discussion session:

Don't get involved in a heated argument over one pet idea. The main purpose in this discussion is to weigh and evaluate various proposals as coolly and reasonably as possible. If you're too emotionally involved, that could be deadly to good judgment.

On the other hand, no one should give in on a point of deep conviction just in order to avoid a verbal battle. If somebody attacks an idea you like, meet him or her head on and stick to your guns until you can be convinced otherwise by reason and logic.

Learn to appreciate differences of opinion. If everybody thinks the same way, you'll never come up with any final solution that's worthwhile. Often, if two people or two factions can't agree on a point, it may be that the best solution is some compromise approach. Usually, reasonable and objective people don't disagree violently about a point unless there's good reason for it. If you can resolve deep internal disagreements early on, it's likely that you'll also avoid a lot of problems that could arise when you begin to implement the ideas agreed upon.

Beware of a quick consensus right at the beginning of your discussion. Usually, if everybody agrees all at once, this means that you simply haven't thought through everything.

Really go for a consensus! Avoid conflict-creating measures like deciding by majority vote or encouraging a member of the group to cave in when he or she really feels strongly about something. Whenever there's an impasse, you can assume that the group simply doesn't have sufficient information. So go out and *get* that information—don't cut off discussion!*

This, then, is a brief outline of some of the principles and steps to follow in setting up a consensus decision-making system in your company. But how exactly will it work out in the real world?

Consider a crisis that a major farm equipment company faced with one of its tractor engines. To stop production on the tractors would have cost them a million dollars a month, and they tried everything they could think of with their engineers, managers and outside consultants to solve the problem. But they just couldn't figure it out.

Then we set up a Shared Participation program with ninety of their key people. The participants included representatives from top management, middle management, engineering, production, supervisory levels and a variety of other areas in the company.

We organized these people into the five-person teams that we've been discussing in the preceding pages—and the problem was solved in just one day.

It turned out that there were three mechanical things which were causing the engine failure, including difficulties with the oiling of the engine shafts and the positioning of the bearings. The difficulty that the company had had in trying to resolve the problem without Shared Participation was that if one of their experts missed one of the flaws, he would completely miss the solution. And the engines would continue to fail. But with ninety heads working together, the total solution emerged in record time!

Nor is the Shared Participation procedure limited to business and industry. An important law enforcement official enrolled in one of our Shared Participation workshops in Michigan. When he came into the program, he said he was convinced that the main purpose and mission of his police department was to arrest suspects. And the police officers under him carried out this mission with a vengeance!

His department had one of the highest arrest rates in the

---

* For further information on these concepts, see *The Art of Sharing,* by Warren E. Avis (New York: Cornerstone Library, 1974).

area, but he had also created as many human relations problems as he had solved. In fact, one of the reasons he came to our workshop was that he was feeling under siege because of hostile attitudes among many public-minded citizens in his area. In addition, there was disaffection in his own police ranks.

As it happened, he got into a Shared Participation discussion group which included a number of people who were active in their communities. Fortunately, they also had some understanding of their local law enforcement agencies.

After he had presented the problem he was facing, the group went through the procedure we've just described above: Each person first submitted five suggested solutions to the problem. Then, they engaged in a discussion to come to a consensus.

After the workshop, this law enforcement official left with a completely new understanding of the function that his department should be serving. Also, he had come up with some ideas about how he could resolve the community relations problems he was facing. He had actually begun to see the situation in his community not just from a police point of view, but also from the broader perspective of the civilian population.

Sure enough, when he got home this official assembled a group of police officers and community leaders and put them through a Shared Participation procedure. Their assignment: Find out ways that the police department might be changed for the better.

The results have been near miraculous—at least they may *seem* miraculous to those who have had no experience with consensus decision making. The police officers in that community have now developed a reputation as "keepers of the peace" and "promoters of the general welfare"—rather than simply as hard-nosed, brutal "nab 'em and jail 'em" cops.

The Shared Participation approach to management and decison making can work equally well in the corporate community. But sometimes, to understand just how well it works, it's helpful first to examine how a business can fall apart without it.

One company based in New York City made a decision that's been common in large metropolitan areas in recent years—they decided to move lock, stock and barrel to the suburbs. The problem with this outfit, however, was that management came to a unilateral decision from the top and then tried to impose it, with no room for discussion or compromise, on all the employees.

In some cases, this approach may succeed in spite of itself. That is, some people will go along with such a high-handed maneuver just because they need the work. Or perhaps they've worked with the company so long they've become victims of inertia.

But in this case, the result was mass revolution. Most employees, with few exceptions, resigned immediately after being presented with the ultimatum!

The chief executive officer and his top advisers were stunned: "How could they possibly do this?" one of the senior executives asked.

The answer is easy. You just can't force a decision without warning on people and expect them in every case to agree to a radical uprooting of their lives. Still, this company went ahead with the move, and it managed to survive—but not without severe disruptions in its operations and a near-catastrophic cut in profits.

What would have been the best way to handle this move? That's an easy one: The lower-level employees should have been brought in on the decision!

This more reasonable and understanding approach was employed by another company that had to make a similar move from a large urban center. In this case, they didn't follow to the letter our concept of Shared Participation. But they did engage in a rather sophisticated form of consensus decision making, so that considerable numbers of people from various interest groups in the company engaged in dialogue with the management.

Most important of all, no effort was made to impose a decision on anybody from the top. Rather, the management people listened carefully to everything that was said. Also, they insisted that there had to be a general agreement about the approach to the move before any concrete steps would be taken to shift the headquarters of the organization.

This particular approach to decision making also involved disseminating information that the lower-level employees weren't aware of.

For example, many didn't realize what a huge percentage of the company's expenses were going into the rental of office space. Also, extensive efforts had been made by the company to negotiate a better rent arrangement with their current landlords, but that had failed. Management had also explored possible leases at other locations in the city, but those didn't work out either.

The only answer from the management's in-depth research seemed to be a move to one of the suburbs. Otherwise, there would be less money available for staff raises and benefits, not to mention profits that could be poured back into the company.

When the employees were presented with such a detailed description of the crisis facing the company, they were quite sympathetic. They sensed their management was really concerned about them. Many elected to take the management's suggestion and move to a new location often cheaper, with better living conditions, and closer to work.

Much of what we've been saying in this chapter may run counter to your image of yourself as the hotshot, wheeling-and-dealing, lone ranger entrepreneur. But believe me, you can't turn unsound preconceptions about macho independence and personal power into a big success.

Certainly, you need a great deal of initiative, personal perseverance and, in many cases, individual brilliance to get a new enterprise off the ground. In fact, in America, it's still possible to be a hero. You can go from rags to riches, if you just have the guts, gumption and grit, and toss in a fair sprinkling of specific know-how.

But to transform your operation from a respectable small success into a big-time, multimillion dollar empire, you have to move beyond the lone ranger mentality. You may always remain a renegade industrial pirate at heart. But if you want to hit your full stride and reach your greatest potential, you must become a pirate *king*—with at least as large a loyal retinue as the Gilbert and Sullivan lead swashbuckler, Richard, in *Pirates of Penzance*.

Developing an appropriate management style is only a part of what it takes to put together a successful large operation. Let's consider a few other important business formulas that can go a long way toward ensuring your ultimate success.

Eleven

Yes, There Is a Formula for Success

"Years mature into fruit
So that some small seeds of moments
May outlive them."

> —*Rabindranath Tagore,*
> On Visiting Yale University, *1932*

I'm always leery of anyone who claims, "Step right up—I've got the secret formula that will grow hair on your head . . . cure your constipation . . . or make you a million dollars overnight!"

Yet I do believe that it's possible—in fact, *essential*—to find some simple, overarching principles for the entrepreneur to follow as he confronts the storms that buffet any new business. In short, it's important to come up with a formula which you can use as a guide. Any good formula should be simple, without being overly simplistic. I like to think of this formula for entrepreneurial success in terms of three major imperatives:

- The basic entrepreneurial imperative: Always focus on service, quality, ingenuity and efficiency;
- The management imperative: Mix young Turks with gray hair; and
- The expense imperative: Be scientific about your allocation of expenses.

In effect, you can regard these statements as exhortations or commands that you regularly give to yourself to help you stay on the right track.

THE BASIC ENTREPRENEURIAL IMPERATIVE: ALWAYS FOCUS ON SERVICE, QUALITY, AESTHETICS, INGENUITY AND EFFICIENCY

Generally speaking, the degree of your success as an entrepreneur is going to depend directly on how good and far-reaching a reputation you can establish. And your reputation will be built on (1) the kind of service you can give; (2) the quality of your product; (3) your ingenuity in developing new products and approaches to the marketplace; and (4) the efficiency of your operation.

If you can develop a reputation for excellent *service*, you're already halfway to success in many fields.

In computers, for example, service is really the name of the game in securing big customers. Business people who are knowledgeable about computers know that the difference between success and failure with a computerized office is often the level of service that the computer company is able to offer.

That's a major reason that some of the big-name brands have been able to do so well. Even a small business with only one or two moderately priced pieces of computer hardware can usually get excellent service from certain established companies simply by paying a standard yearly service fee. The service charge may be high—as much as $500 a year for one medium-sized piece of equipment. But plenty of small operators are willing to pay, so long as they can be sure their personal computer, electronic typewriter or word processor will be fixed within a matter of hours, on the same day that it goes "down."

In short, smart people are willing to pay more if they can just get good service for the item they buy. It's wise for business executives to keep this fact in mind as they try to develop an excellent reputation in a community.

The *quality* of your product is also a key factor. You've got to field-test it thoroughly so that you're sure that all the "gremlins" have been eliminated. Also, be sure that you emphasize quality control over each item that you ship out so that each consumer item is in proper working order.

In a recent report in one of the financial publications, an investigation of the software that was being put out by leaders in the field revealed that there were many "gliches," or defects, in some of the most expensive business programs. That sort of thing certainly doesn't help a corporation's public image! In fact, an article or two of this type can actually sound the death knell for an enterprise.

Quality may also involve *aesthetics*—or the physical "look" of an item. With some products, of course, like big main-frame computers, prospective buyers really don't care that much how they look. Consumers are more concerned about how they work and how well they're serviced.

But the appeal of other products, such as automobiles, may depend heavily on outward appearance. In this case, people may try to separate the veneer, or "look," of a product from its underlying quality. But the two factors may be so intimately connected that they often can't be separated in the minds of potential buyers.

Aesthetics can be just as important when you're making a presentation for a service-oriented enterprise. Suppose your venture involves selling some financial product like insurance, or perhaps giving some sort of face-to-face advice. In that case, you'll find you must pay very careful attention to cultivating an image that suggests the high quality of what you have to offer.

In this regard, I'm reminded of one very successful pension, insurance and investment-counseling company in a large northeastern city. The staff made its main sales pitch with a slick but comprehensive computerized analysis of each client's financial position. Using a lecture-style presentation in a paneled board room, with the prospective client as the only one in the "audience," two members of the staff explained the program, offered support and answered questions.

In this case, the actual, underlying "products," which included advice, insurance and other investment vehicles, were certainly of high quality. But just as important as the products and services was the classy way in which they were presented.

In a recent survey from *Chain-Store Age* magazine, reported in *The Wall Street Journal* (October 4, 1985), consumers were asked what they considered to be the most important factors in determining the value of a piece of merchandise. Their responses say a great deal about the attitude of the American public toward the quality and aesthetics of a business product: workmanship was cited as a key factor by 23 percent; price by 21 percent; materials by 14 percent; and the "looks" of an item by 13 percent.

Also, it's important to include *ingenuity* as a part of the "basic entrepreneurial imperative." Being on the cutting edge of your field is essential if you hope to hit the top levels of success.

In some high-tech fields you may have to produce the most advanced product in the field if you hope to stake out a strong position in the marketplace. But ingenuity, originality and uniqueness have an important place in *any* company. So, if you sell insurance, you'd better have the most up-to-date presentation of your financial products and also offer the latest financial products.

Finally, there's the imperative of *efficiency*. You must manage the office, produce the product, and otherwise run the company so that you can minimize your costs and thus maximize your profits. The low-cost, high-quality operator, who is also a superior merchandiser, is usually the winner.

Your level of efficiency will also have a direct bearing on how well you can "penetrate" your chosen marketplace. In other words, with an efficient operation and low overhead and expenses, you'll be able to keep the price of your product or service at the lowest possible profit level. In turn, you'll be able to offer your products or services at competitive rates, and your pool of prospective customers—as well as your profits—should increase proportionately.

THE MANAGEMENT IMPERATIVE:
MIX YOUNG TURKS WITH GRAY HAIR

In a previous section of this book, we've seen how many new ventures fail because they lack what I call gray hair—or old-fashioned experience—in responsible management positions. But there's more to be said on this subject.

Most entrepreneurial ventures are put together by young Turks who have the energy, enthusiasm and creativity necessary to get a new venture off the ground.

But if you just have a bunch of young kids who may be quite bright and have a lot of enthusiasm but who completely lack business experience, they'll certainly make some horrendous blunders. That's why so many new enterprises fail, even when they have great products.

It's also why most seasoned venture capital people will say, before they put their money into a new concept, "We've got to have some managerial control." In effect, they're saying, "We want the right to bring in some gray hair."

If you think about it for a moment, it just makes good sense: Any new venture is going to be stronger if there are one or more top people who can confront a tough new problem by saying: "I've been through this before. From my own experience, I can tell you that here's what's likely to work . . . and here's what's likely to fail."

On the other hand, the founder of the company—who usually has the big ideas and the capacity to motivate others—may be able to get along without the caution and even-handedness that age can bestow. In fact, if the entrepreneur has been around too long, he may lack guts. He may be constitutionally incapable of taking the risks necessary to catapult a new business concept into big-time success.

In short, too much gray hair can make a company stodgy and immobile. Also, many people with much experience in what can go wrong with a new venture may become battle weary. They tend to think in terms of what *can't* be done, rather than what the possibilities are with a new business project. In short, they may lack the entrepreneurial spirit that it takes to get a new venture off the ground.

Recently, in a conversation about whether or not a new company should be given venture capital money, there was some disagreement about whether the basic concept would be able to succeed. Finally, one of the participants made the decisive point.

He said, "You want to know what the potential of this company is? Look at the management. They've all got one foot in the grave!" That convinced everyone that the company should *not* receive funds.

In other words, having too many seasoned old pros is as bad as not having any gray hair at all. It takes the combination of young Turks and gray hair to make a company go. A good balance between hot-blooded enthusiasm and solid experience can make the difference between success and failure in the early stages of any venture. For that matter, these principles are valid for any business, new or old.

So who in a company should have the gray hair? In most

cases, your general manager should have had years of experience. Otherwise, he's likely to make so many errors along the way that survival of the company during tough times may become impossible. A good manager needs at least ten years of experience and preferably closer to fifteen to understand how to oversee an enterprise. It takes that long to learn how to resolve the dozens of daily problems that arise in a business.

It's also important for the person in charge of production to have a broad, practical personal history in a production-oriented area. You want somebody who has made his mistakes with other companies. He should be prepared when you hire him to apply his rich background to your venture.

On the other hand, if you pull in an inexperienced production person and in effect give him on-the-job training with your company, he may go away with a lot of important knowledge. But *you* will be the one who suffers most from his inexperience.

Finally, it's helpful to have someone on board who has been through the wars in corporate finance. If you can find an expert who really understands financial cost control, you'll be well on the way to making the most out of every dollar you bring in.

The contrast between companies that have too much "gray hair" on the one hand, and too little on the other, can be striking.

One company which had plenty of old-timers but no vibrant young people in key management positions was one of the most frustrating outfits imaginable. They had a good product and were making a small profit. But in general, the revenues of the company had been fairly flat over a period of years.

Every time our venture capital division, which had made substantial investment in the operation, would question the management about their failure to improve their performance, we always heard the same story. In response to a suggestion about a way to help their performance, the manager's answer would go something like this: "That's a nice idea. But you know, I've seen that tried before, and it has its limitations. Why, when I was in such-and-such a company. . . . "

In other words, you have to be wary of people who are locked into their past experience. They always tell you about the failures, but not about the great successes of other companies in the business. They usually become set in their ways—and they may very well miss entire markets because they're operating with blinders from the distant past. They fail to realize that times *do* change, and so the ways we respond to new challenges must also change, at least to some degree.

Young hotshots, in contrast, tend to see the new markets. They may also have an excellent idea about what the potential of a new product can be. But more often than not, if they are left to operate by themselves, they'll start heading off in all sorts of different directions. And that can kill an enterprise just as surely as can a gaggle of gray hairs.

This problem also plagued another company—one in which, to my great regret, I failed to secure a 51 percent interest. As a result, I didn't have control. So I had to stand on the sidelines and watch a group of young fellows practically destroy the place before it dawned on them what they were doing.

They were whirling in a dozen directions. For example, they had set up an advertising campaign and spent $100,000 to get it going. But then the young president and his inexperienced advertising manager got into an argument about how to run the final stages of the advertising strategy.

Specifically, the advertising manager wanted to spend $200,000 on a one-shot advertising deal. The president, a visionary "idea man" with little experience in marketing, thought that didn't sound quite right. But he couldn't make up his mind about what *was* right.

As a result, they argued and discussed this issue for five months, and during that period they didn't run any ads at all. Consequently, their sales stagnated, the initial expenditures on their advertising budget were largely wasted, and the company began to suffer huge losses.

Clearly, all this company needed was a little gray hair with experience to set the advertising and marketing strategy back on the right track. As the outside venture capitalist, we finally managed to get the company's leadership to listen to some consultants, who temporarily filled the need for gray hair in management.

Of course, in suggesting you pull in a perfect mix of experience and entrepreneurial energy, I'm talking about the ideal situation. When you first start off your new venture, you may not have the money or the contacts to hire experienced experts in all these fields.

But, as a basic principle, the key thing to keep in mind is a proper balance between youthful, entrepeneurial enthusiasm and the level-headed, hands on experience that comes with age.

Also, a person's age is never a matter of mere chronology: Someone quite young chronologically may be quite old and even ossified in spirit, and a person relatively advanced in years may be quite youthful in the way he or she deals with new concepts and issues. Certainly, chronological age may provide some indication of a person's probable energy levels, freshness of thought and especially of experience. But when you are evaluating potential employees or partners, delve a little more deeply into their emotional buoyancy and mental quickness.

In my own case, I often have trouble acknowledging my age because I feel younger than I really am. Also, the big issue of age intensifies at the end of each decade of my life. When I reached thirty, for example, I got concerned because I thought I was "getting on in years." When I hit forty, I couldn't believe that I was so ancient: I really felt as young as I had back in my twenties, when I was just putting the Avis Airlines Rent-A-Car concept together.

And age fifty? That was really hard to take! I was unable to remain in the Young Presidents Organization anymore, and that was a real shock. You're out at fifty! It took me nearly ten years to face up to the fact that I had passed the fifty-year milestone. I even avoided some top executive organizations, like Chief Executive Forum, because I felt they were too old for me!

The same sort of age-related trauma has bothered me periodically in ensuing years because I never felt as old in body or spirit as I was in years.

As someone has said: "Youth is not a time of life; It's a state of mind."

THE EXPENSE IMPERATIVE: BE SCIENTIFIC ABOUT YOUR ALLOCATION OF EXPENSES

One of the biggest mistakes most entrepreneurs make is that they fail to keep their expenses under control. In the early phases of any new venture, the name of the game is growth. You want to sell as much as you can; open as many markets as you can; and keep your production machinery going in high gear.

The most aggressive, and usually the most successful, entrepreneurs are always ready to respond when a new customer appears on the horizon—as long as it's possible to sell profitably to that newcomer. I'm a great believer in focusing on growth. One thing that I always want in business is to have too many orders. We'll take more orders than we know how to handle. Then, one way or another, we'll learn how to solve that problem. It's when there isn't enough business that I begin to get worried.

But at some point, you've got to stand back and put your house in order. That means doing a thorough, systematic, scientific analysis of the costs and expenses and management capabilities in your company.

Obviously, it's not possible to lay down one and only one formula for expenses that will apply perfectly to every business venture. In some industries, such as the high-tech field, you can expect net income to be higher than the norm—say 10-20 percent or even more. But if you'll try to do a better job of controlling your expenses, you'll be taking a giant step toward maximizing your profits. It may only take a small increase in your expenses—sometimes as little as 1 percent or less in seven or eight different categories—to turn a profit into a loss.

The importance of keeping a close watch on expenses was impressed on me once again recently as I was evaluating my horse farm. A number of business friends who came in to take a look said they regarded the operation as quite well run.

In fact, one said, "Warren, I don't believe you could save another hundred dollars a month on this operation, no matter how hard you try."

But I wasn't convinced. So I itemized all the expenses and had them plugged into detailed, computerized spread sheets. The results were absolutely phenomenal. Just by trimming a little here and a little there from the various parts of the enterprise we were able to save $4,000 to $5,000 a month on the farm.

Here's how it worked:

First of all, as we examined all our equipment, we saw we had a number of unnecessary cars. Because we had written them off on our tax returns, we were fooled into thinking they were costing us very little. But when we looked more closely, we saw that in fact they were costing us $3,000 to $4,000 a year! The total included a few hundred dollars for insurance and several hundred dollars each on repair bills and various other expenses.

Ironically, those extra cars were rarely used. They weren't included at all in our expenses for oil and gas! By getting rid of them, we were well on our way to a significant increase in our profits.

Then, we began to look at our energy expenses. One of the first things that caught our eye was an extra conference room which we heated, but which was never used during the winter. The heat for that space was running about $300 a month on the average. So, we shut the heat off and saved several thousand a year.

The farm also has a heated swimming pool, which is usually in use only in the summer. Still, we found that the pool was being heated all the time, at an expense averaging $250 a month. So we decided to turn the heaters off. Also, we installed a special solar cover and insulation system which would hold the heat for longer periods of time. These improvements resulted in considerable savings.

As we studied other facilities on the farm, we noticed there was one large office which was rarely in use, even though it was constantly being heated. At this point we decided the best way to stop such waste would be to install thermostats and meters in each room. In the past, we had only one thermostat for the entire building. Before long, it became apparent that this measure was going to save us a tremendous amount of money—including about $600 a month just on our decision to reduce heat on that one large office that wasn't being used, except for occasional meetings.

I got so excited about the savings we were achieving that I became almost obsessed with eliminating every flaw that we had in our energy setup. But one item was still puzzling: During the summer, we were getting monthly gas heating bills for about $100, even though we didn't have the heat turned on. We simply couldn't figure out where this expense was coming from.

Finally, after considerable investigation, we discovered that we had a big hot-water heater which was constantly turned on, even during long periods when it wasn't used. So we turned it down when nobody was there and saved just that much more money. Also, we avoid lapsing back into the same mistake because now we keep control of these items on our computerized expense spread sheets. They "flash" any change from our expense forecasts.

Apart from the energy problems, there were also plenty of other expense inefficiencies and loopholes. One of the biggest was the misuse of our company credit cards.

We had established a system with several credit cards for our employees to use to get gas for company cars. But when we examined the breakdown of expenses for this item, we noticed that they seemed extremely high.

Upon further investigation, we discovered that a number of people were filling up their *own* cars at the gas station as they went home at night. Obviously, our system of controlling those credit cards wasn't very effective! As a result, we pulled in all the cards and established a more effective means of controlling them. That step, as well, saved us hundreds of dollars a year.

So when we put all the savings on the farm together, they came to $4,000 to $5,000 per month. That amounts to $50,000 to $60,000 a year on a relatively small operation!

I took this lesson to heart, and I would advise any other entrepreneur to do the same. The main idea is to be systematic and scientific as you formulate the expense picture for your own company. Make sure you have two years of monthly expense sheets available. Then, sit down with your people and a list of expenses, and ask yourselves questions like these:

- Do any of these expenses seem unusually high?
- Have we left out any major areas where we're spending money to run the business?
- How can we make some cuts in expenditures—even if they amount to only a few dollars?

In answering that last question, I'd recommend that you and your staff go over each expense item and meditate on it for a few months. You'll be surprised at how many ideas for streamlining your operation will come from your team.

I don't pretend that these three "imperatives" are enough in themselves to make your venture a great success. But they are part of a healthy, succinct formula which will keep you focused on the issues that will help you succeed. If you think about it for a moment, most of the key ingredients to success are contained in the overall formula:

- Good service
- High quality
- Aesthetics
- Ingenuity
- Efficiency
- A balance between experience and exuberant youth
- Streamlined expenses on spread sheets

Still, even if you follow all the rules and principles and do everything that's humanly possible to turn your business into a success, you're bound to run into problems. And some of those problems may well bring you into contact with lawyers or may even land you in court. Now, let's examine a few basic principles that will help you stay *out* of court.

Twelve

This Side of the Law

"The first thing we do, let's kill all the lawyers."

—William Shakespeare,
Henry VI, *Part II*,
Act IV, Scene 2

*L*ike many people of our own time, William Shakespeare definitely didn't like lawyers.

And it's certainly true that too many lawyers and lawsuits can be the bane of anyone's existence.

But at the same time, I think it's a big mistake for any executive or entrepreneur to be ignorant of the way that the law and lawyers work. You can save yourself a tremendous amount of time, aggravation and money if you can just find a good attorney to guide you through the twists and turns of litigation and negotiation.

But how do you find the right lawyer?

Certainly, it's not easy. In general, I think it's much easier to get a good accountant than it is a good lawyer. The wrong adviser in either of these fields can foul up your business so badly that you may feel like throwing in the towel and starting all over again. But a top-flight legal or accounting adviser can make your life in the legal lane livable.

When you're looking for a lawyer, there are several things to keep in mind:

Ask prospective attorneys for references and check them out. If possible, find some successful business people in your community that you trust, and ask *them* to refer you to their lawyers.

Evaluate your would-be lawyer's track record. Has he represented many reputable clients? Do they stick with him over a long period of time? How has he come out in the courtroom and in the negotiation of settlements? And perhaps the most important question of all: Does he have the reputation of being a deal*maker* or a deal*breaker*?

Be sure to pick a specialist when one is needed. A law firm may tell you that they're good in everything, but you can be sure that they're *really* good only in certain areas. So, if you're looking for advice on a patent issue, be sure to get a patent lawyer. Or, a firm may have a preponderance of its accounts in real estate; and that means if *you're* in real estate, you should hire that type of firm. You don't want to use your patent lawyer for this type of work. By the same token, if you're dealing with a merger or acquisition problem, you should find an attorney who specializes in mergers and acquisitions. You'll also probably want to use one type of lawyer for negotiations and another type for litigation.

One of the biggest problems that arises in dealing with lawyers is picking the wrong attorney to do a particular job.

When you first hire an attorney, regard the relationship as being on a temporary, case-by-case basis. Despite the fact that the law requires a lot of rather specialized knowledge, you shouldn't leave your common sense at your law firm's door. If his answers to you are always vague or noncommital, that may mean he isn't very well versed or perhaps isn't even very bright. A lawyer should inspire confidence and make you feel comfortable; if he doesn't, that's a good sign that you should look elsewhere for legal advice.

Your lawyer should always have time for you. All accomplished professionals are going to be in great demand, and that means that their time is at a premium. Certainly, if you walk into a lawyer's office and it's evident that nobody else has been using him, you would be justified in questioning whether he's entirely competent.

On the other hand, if he never seems to have time to return your calls or to meet with you, then I'd be wary of hiring him. Even the best lawyer is not going to do you any good unless he's available to give you advice, guidance and support.

Be aggressive in inquiring about fees and hourly rates. As a client, you have every right to ask your attorney (or your accountant, for that matter) to give you a full explanation about how he arrives at the cost of his services. Lawyers charge by the hour, and so you should ascertain exactly what their rate is— whether the cost of a specific job is negotiable. Also, feel free to ask for a regular, itemized bill showing exactly what you're being charged for and how the dollar figures are computed.

Finally, when you've settled on a lawyer, cultivate a real friend-

ship. Good and *regular* legal counsel can save you thousands—or even millions—of dollars. From personal experience, I've learned that one line in a contract may turn out to be crucial later. A bit of sound legal strategy at the beginning of a business negotiation can pay off handsomely when problems begin to develop in a business deal.

As a result, it's important to find a good attorney as early as possible in your business venture. That way, you'll be more likely to anticipate legal difficulties ahead of time, and you'll also be in a position to hit the ground running if you get slapped with a lawsuit.

It's almost impossible to prepare yourself psychologically in advance for legal combat. Quite frankly, it used to drive me crazy when an enexpected lawsuit would arise. But over the years, I've learned to expect the unexpected on the legal front, and now I'm psychologically adjusted. I'm prepared in my inner being, as well as in my choice of attorneys, to deal with legal challenges. That makes it a great deal easier to stay calm during the turmoil of legal shenanigans.

One lawsuit which was certainly unexpected, but which I was emotionally and legally prepared to handle, dealt with the Avis name. When I sold Avis Rent-A-Car, I didn't sell the name "Avis" for any purpose other than the rent-a-car business. That was clear in the contract of sale.

But then, I was introduced to the world of corporate guerrilla fighting. The problems began when I set up a flower business called Avis Flowers Worldwide.

The concept involved establishing a direct 800 number which customers could call to buy flowers. This enterprise was also tied in with another business, called Teleflorist, in which I was a major owner. With the Teleflorist system, you could order flowers through one florist in one part of town or the country. Then, that florist would arrange for the delivery via the Teleflorist system by another florist miles away. In other words, we serviced florists around the country by clearing their transactions between cities. Teleflorist was the second largest firm of its kind, next to FTD.

At the new Avis Flowers operation, we had thought we were great friends with the Avis Rent-A-Car Company, as we always had been in the past. In fact, we invited executives from Avis to our opening day party. Then, the next day we were served with a subpoena.

The then-owners of Avis Rent-A-Car, the Norton Simon Company, had decided that despite a prior contract—which clearly stated they only had the right to the Avis name for the rent-a-car operation—they didn't want me to use my own name in this retail business. So, they decided to use the old corporate trick of slapping a smaller operator with a lawsuit that would easily cost up to $200,000.

It didn't matter that the big corporation would probably lose. The danger to the little guy was that his legal fees would become too burdensome for him to stay in business. The cost of the suit would usually break the small operator.

But what Norton Simon had failed to count on was that I had chosen my lawyers at least as well as they had theirs. Also, I had the money to stay with them through a lengthy legal action. Finally, I was so furious that I didn't care what it cost—I was determined to fight them to the end, on principle if nothing else!

So I met them head-on in federal court. And they lost—even though they tried to do an end run around our contract by relying on a federal act, the Lanham Act, which prohibits confusion between names of businesses. In other words, they attempted to use a federal law to invalidate a legal contract.

The judge took a look at what they were trying to do, wrote a scathing opinion against them, and threw the case out of court. He said, in effect, that it didn't make sense to think people were going to believe they were renting a car when they were actually buying flowers. That would be an insult to the intelligence of the American public!

After their suit was dismissed, I immediately brought another suit for $200 million against Norton Simon and settled for millions of dollars out of court.

But even though I came out on top in these legal actions, that doesn't mean that I didn't get hurt. The court case dragged out for a year and a half, and it put us in the position of not knowing whether we were in the Avis Flowers business or not.

There was a ripple effect that rocked my other affairs as well: The lawsuit caused problems between me and my partners in the Teleflorist company. A major problem was that my Teleflorist partners, who had nothing to do with running Avis Flowers, found themselves embroiled in depositions and subpoenas.

Finally, it became evident that the Avis Flowers concept had been wrecked by the lawsuit. I got so disgusted with the whole business that I also sold my interest in Teleflorist.

Teleflorist is still doing very well, and we made millions on the sale. But despite the fact that I came out extremely well financially, both in the lawsuit with Norton Simon and also in the sale of Teleflorist, the experience left a sour taste in my mouth. Litigation is simply not a pleasant way to do business.

Legally speaking, I was well protected. I had made proper preparations for the unexpected, and those preparations paid off in the end. But lawsuits and legalities of any type should always be regarded as the last resort. You don't get into business to fight and destroy; you get into it to create. Lawyers and their protective devices can help protect you from worst-case scenarios. But if you have a choice, it's always best to stay completely out of legal hassles and courtroom battles.

The impact of a legal challenge can be even more devastating if you're not too well prepared. In one company a number of years ago, we produced a very effective summer product, and before long we were up to $5 million in sales. Also, a major company began to run ads promoting the product, and it seemed that the sky would be the limit.

The whole thing was an entrepreneur's dream—except for one fatal flaw. The root of the problem lay in the fact that the product was only good for summer business. If we wanted to produce it ourselves, that meant that we also needed a winter product. But nothing captured our interest at that particular time. As a result, we got another company, which made a winter item, to manufacture the product, and that proved to be our undoing.

Our big mistake was to allow this other company to assemble all our parts and also to ship the product to our customers. We even spent a half million dollars teaching this company how to produce and distribute the product! As a result, they had access to our total business operation—and they made the most profitable use of it.

The upshot was that this subcontractor set up their own company and began to put out a similar product. We brought a patent suit against them, but we soon found that we couldn't win because of a technicality: The former owners had failed to file for a patent within a certain period of time, as required by law, after the product had hit the market.

So I was boxed into a corner. The best that we could do was to sell the subcontractor the rest of our company, just to get some salvage value out of the inventory. The whole thing was a disaster, and it cost a great deal of money.

But I did learn some valuable lessons.

First of all, I learned how important it is to be in touch with a good patent lawyer when you're setting up a business involving a new product. You can lose it all if you don't take the proper filing steps required by the government.

Also, we learned to pay closer attention to mapping out a production strategy to protect ourselves from legal complications.

Specifically, we should never have put such total control of the production of our product in the hands of one outside company. This allowed the outsiders to learn too much about our product and business. We should have reserved the right to do the final assembly ourselves; also, we should have kept control of our customer list. The development of a strategy along these lines requires good legal counsel; and it also involves a reliance on sound business principles and just good common sense.

Certainly, I regret this experience deeply. But at the same time, I'm glad that we decided to cut our losses and move on to something else. It's all very aggravating, to feel that you've been stabbed in the back by a business colleague. But you can't spend your entire business life in lawsuits. When somebody has you over a barrel, even if you feel you're the victim of an injustice, the best thing is to get up and start on something new.

Still, I regret the drift of our business culture toward more litigation. I've always preferred doing business simply on a handshake, with personal contacts whom I feel I can trust. That's the way I operated with the airlines when I first started out with the rent-a-car company. But then, attitudes began to change, and with one recent proposal, I discovered to my chagrin that handshakes were not the way you did business anymore.

My basic idea was simple. Through my own extensive travel, I had seen what a problem the airlines face in tracing lost baggage and trying to deliver it speedily to irate passengers. My concept was to streamline the process and set up an umbrella system to handle the lost baggage problem for *all* the airlines.

The main idea was to make every piece of baggage as identifiable as possible and then to revolutionize the system of running down and delivering lost pieces of baggage. We proposed *requiring* that one standard tag, identifying the passenger by name, address and telephone number, be attached to every bag. No baggage would be accepted without the tag. (Remember: At this time, no name tags were required.) Then, right after a flight's baggage was unloaded, an airline attendant would gather the tag information from all unclaimed bags. This information would then be sent right out to our central baggage control center.

Even if the lost bag had not already been reported missing to our center by the passenger (who might still be in transit), we would contact the passenger's office or home by telephone. In many cases we expected to be able to get the lost bag to his destination before he even arrived! Or if we had received a lost bag complaint already, we would find the bag and send it out immediately to the passenger's destination on the next plane, regardless of airline.

Under our proposal, the passenger who found that his bag had not arrived with his flight would only have to check in with an airline attendant at the lost and found department. He would not need to fill out any additional forms or wait for hours to make his report.

According to our studies, we could have saved the airlines millions of dollars in lost or mishandled baggage. Also, we were certain that we would be able to minimize passenger complaints and frustrations. Our entire system had been designed to get the passenger and his baggage back together in the shortest possible time.

Although this proposal was submitted to the airlines, they rejected it. Then we took it to the Civil Aeronautics Board and they seemed to like it and indicated they would contact the airlines. We thought that sounded great, but finally, without even notifying us or giving us credit, the CAB decided to make use of the proposal which suggested requiring a record of name, address and telephone number.

Certainly, it disappointed me that the CAB and the airlines weren't willing to get together on an industry-wide program. It was doubly disturbing that they would take my idea and use it as though they had thought of it themselves. In addition, I was annoyed that various airlines simply picked up on our ideas and incorporated them into their systems without giving us any credit or compensation. They actually told the CAB they had thought of the concepts before! They probably had, but had never been able to convince the CAB to implement them nationally. To ward off such piracy, I finally got into the habit of including a paragraph in my proposals that read like this:

> The process is submitted for your review in confidence, with the understanding that the confidential disclosures are made for the purpose of subsequent negotiation. Avis Research Center does not abandon its proprietary interest in these systems.

But of course, you can never protect yourself completely from people who want to take your ideas and proposals and make them their own. You can only go so far with cautionary paragraphs, legal conditions and contractual clauses. Consider what happened with another proposal that I made—an idea for expediting the shipment of small parcels on passenger flights.

Beginning in 1966, we began to develop a small package service system for use by domestic airlines. The main idea, similar to concepts later used by Federal Express, was to speed the delivery of such items as cancelled checks, legal documents, emergency parts and scientific instruments. The items were to be transported in suitcases or other containers of a standard size so they would be small and light enough to be handled like ordinary passenger baggage.

We put a great deal of time, effort, research and money into the development of this system. Then, in 1969, we made a formal presentation to an airline. As was our custom, we told the officials at the airline that we were discussing this proposal with them in confidence. It was our understanding that we would pay the start-up costs, run it for them, and have the responsibility for pickup and delivery of the packages and for establishing a pricing schedule. If the package system was adopted, we would be appropriately compensated through profit sharing.

During the next six months, I met with a representative of the airline on almost a monthly basis to discuss the adoption and implementation of this small package service system. Finally, in the spring of 1970, they asked me to write up a detailed description of the proposed service, so that other officials could evaluate it.

Although I went along with this request, I was in for a rude shock. Several weeks later, I met with several executives, who informed me that there wasn't enough of a market for my proposed system, even though the baggage compartments were 80 percent empty at that time. They said, in effect, "It's not feasible, it's uneconomical and it won't work. Also, we'd have union problems."

Then came the big surprise. In the fall of 1970, the airline instituted nationally a small package service system which was almost identical to the one that I had proposed. I was unhappy, but we finally dropped the matter.

Granted, I was reasonably well prepared legally for the problem that developed. But of course, I never expected to get embroiled in controversy on a deal like this; nor did I expect to spend years on a proposal only to have it used by others.

Rather, like any ambitious entrepreneur, I started out in a completely positive frame of mind. I launched this venture with truly global visions of sugarplums dancing in my head. And I'm sure if my proposal had been accepted, everyone, including the airlines, would have come out ahead. That's essentially what's happened with Federal Express.

So, having the deal fall through was a great disappointment. My getting something out of a legal settlement could never make up for the lost opportunity. I finally concluded that the airlines are becoming like the railroads—out of touch with the realities of the marketplace. In recent years, however, deregulation has made them more aware and creative.

But that's the way life is in the entrepreneurial fast lane. If you come up with a hot idea and then develop it to the point of implementation, there's always a danger that someone's going to step in and try to take it away from you. You can't copyright or otherwise legally protect most ideas—especially while you're still in the planning stages. Consequently, there are innumerable ways that sharp operators can step in and benefit from the fruits of your hard work and thought.

But still, it's possible to put business "big boys" on notice that you're not going to be pushed around. Some of the "principles of protection" may be summarized this way:

Spend some time with your most trusted attorney to map out a strategy to protect yourself and your idea. He'll help you draft letters and protective legal notices that may help to ward off prospective pirates.

Fly plenty of legal "red flags" when you go into a business negotiation. For example, when you write letters to companies suggesting a proposal, you might include a clause like the one mentioned earlier, which we've inserted in some of our proposals.

Of course, it's important to be realistic here. Many companies won't talk to you if you approach them with such a clause. Representatives of the company may have already thought of your idea. In any case, they may not want to be bound by your conditions. On the other hand, they *may* look at your idea, even with the strings you've attached, because they're afraid of missing a great opportunity. This is a dilemma you'll have to resolve with prospective clients on a case-by-case basis.

Build a "paper trail." In other words, as you're negotiating with a prospective client, write letters summarizing the results of conversations and negotiations. It may be helpful to have your lawyer "vet," or read over, this correspondence before you mail it out so that you can close as many legal loopholes as possible. It's also wise to jot down in your daily calendar or on some memo pad your contacts and conversations with various individuals. Your notes should include the content of what was said and the dates and places where the discussions took place.

A related issue—one which relates more to *you* than to potential business adversaries—concerns the importance of conducting an above-board business, with clear, correct records.

Many, many entrepreneurs believe, for example, that it's not possible to get ahead unless you play games with the Internal Revenue Service in the "underground" cash economy. In other words, they argue, it's necessary to engage in cash transactions which you keep "off the books" so that you don't have to report them as income and pay tax on them. Believe me, it's *not* necessary to try to cheat on your taxes in order to achieve success. On the contrary, you're much more likely to end up with heavy fines or behind bars if you engage in such practices.

This point was impressed on me a number of years ago when I decided to sell a boat that I owned. The buyer gave me a $10,000 deposit, which he passed on to me as cash in an envelope. I, in turn, handed it directly to my secretary and told her to enter it on our books. The sale of the boat was consummated shortly afterward, and I didn't think any more about the matter—until two years later when an Internal Revenue Service agent came knocking on my door. It seemed that the man who had bought my boat had been indicted for fraud, and in the course of his interrogation, he had said he had given this $10,000 to me in cash. The IRS now wanted to know what record I had of the money.

While they were in my office, I called my secretary in and said, "Show the agents where the money is entered." But she couldn't find it.

Now, I was beginning to get uncomfortable, especially when I noticed the way the IRS people were looking at me. I actually began to wonder whether or not that money really had been entered on the books, and knew I was in big trouble if it hadn't.

Fortunately, three days later, they found the $10,000 in my ledgers. Of course, the irony here is that I had no intention of trying to get away with anything. But I was impressed again, in a rather dramatic way, with how important it is for *every* entrepreneur or any other person to play the business game according to the rules. This should be the first line of protection in any consideration of the legalities of operating in the American marketplace.

The first time or two that you try to follow these protective measures, you may feel unsure of yourself. Or you may just sense the whole thing is a waste of time. But after you get into the habit of following these guidelines, you'll find that they begin to come quite naturally. And if you ever do end up with a legal problem, believe me, you'll be very happy you've protected your flanks!

No matter how pleasant a prospective client or collaborator may seem at first, problems may arise—just as they do in the best of marriages. Business can be a lot of fun; but it's also a battle-ground. There's plenty of opportunity for sweetness and light *after* you've nailed down a deal and actually launched a venture with a new partner.

It's simply a matter of learning to anticipate the worst, and then getting your lawyer to help you prepare for difficulties. Then, you'll be much more likely to reach a peaceful settlement—or at least walk away from a bad situation with your business interests reasonably intact.

Thirteen

Marvelous Mistakes
I've Made

"Experience is the name everyone gives to his mistakes."
—*Oscar Wilde,* Lady Windermere's Fan, *Act III*

*T*here's always a danger, when one is recounting past exploits and adventures, to fall into the trap of imagined invincibility. In other words, it would be easy for me to try to present myself as the perfect entrepreneur, who has never been guilty of any sort of misstep or stupid decision.

I hope that in the previous pages, you have enough illustrations of my entrepreneurial errors and even near idiocies to disabuse you of any false notions. But just to make sure that you get the point, I'm now going to regale you in greater detail with some of my biggest business blunders.

I readily acknowledge that most of my mistakes and failures have a peculiar Avis brand upon them. In other words, I'll be the first to admit that my shortcomings are not necessarily going to be yours; and conversely, yours won't necessarily be mine. But still, there are some generalizations we can make and also some lessons we can learn from the foolish moves and mishaps of others.

Generally speaking, there are five main reasons why a new business may fail:

(1) Poor management can cause: (2) serious product problems, (3) poor sales effort, and (4) inefficiency; and these difficulties may be further aggravated by (5) bad economic trends.

Many times, the most critical mistakes that entrepreneurs make are related somehow to one or more of these five categories. Sometimes, it's poor management that threatens to sink the ship. Other times, a bad economic situation, either in the nation or in a specific segment of the economy, can do an entrepreneur in. Yet with a little thought and foresight you can easily sidestep many big problems.

Now, let's consider a few of the marvelous and not-so-marvelous mistakes I've made over the years. Then, in the convenient role of Monday-morning quarterbacks, we'll try to decide what I might have done differently.

MISTAKE #1: THE FIFTY-FIFTY DEAL

At one time during my career, I went on an equal partners kick which turned out to be a total disaster. In other words, I would put in most of the money for a venture, and in return I'd receive 50 percent of the business. The other partner, who was usually an entrepreneur with a special idea but with little cash, ended up getting the other 50 percent of the company. He also had the responsibility of managing the day-to-day operations. Unfortunately, the partners were frequently too young and inexperienced; and worst of all, they wouldn't listen to advice.

In every case, without exception, major problems arose, usually as a result of a lack of management experience—and many times the companies went completely out of business. My mistake? I should have asked for 51 percent! That way, when things began to go wrong, my people could have stepped in and taken over control of the situation until the problem was corrected.

For example, I went in even-steven with a real estate entrepreneur who had set up a real estate listing operation in a very promising midwestern metropolitan area. In this case, the real estate man had contributed money, but I also put up some.

During the preliminary negotiations, the other entreprenuer had consistently agreed with me about our mission, goals and strategy. I was very happy about the whole situation because I thought we were completely on the same wavelength. But as it turned out, he was agreeing with me mainly because he wanted money.

It was only after the contract had been signed and the business was moving forward that I discovered we didn't quite see eye-to-eye on everything.

In this situation, the major disagreement was the way that the sales commissions had been structured. He thought that they should be set at a relatively high percentage of the sales prices, while I felt strongly that they should be set much lower. So we reached an impasse, which couldn't be resolved unless one or the other of us completely gave way. Being the ultimate pragmatist, I decided to allow him, as the "hands-on" manager in this situation, to have the last word. He went ahead and did things his way and lost his money as well as mine. So we folded the business.

Obviously, if I had owned 51 percent of the venture, I could have just presented this guy with an ultimatum "Either you buy me out or find another partner!" But having locked myself into a fifty-fifty arrangement, with all the stresses, strains and frustrations which that entailed, I had no alternative but to watch this promising venture go down the tubes.

In a variation on the same fifty-fifty theme, I was approached by a businessman who had developed a self-help instructional series which he felt could make a great deal of money if properly marketed. I agreed, and we formed a corporation in which we each owned 50 percent of the stock and had equal representation on the board of directors. Our arrangement was that he would supply the product; I supplied all the money, including his substantial salary, office rent, telephone, clerical help, salespeople and other support systems.

The project got started with a bang, and we began to make money in short order. But then we ran into a problem. Now that we were successful, my partner decided that he should own more of the company than I did, and he demanded that I relinquish a substantial portion of my interest. Needless to say, I didn't agree. That simply wasn't part of our deal.

My partner's solution? He formed a new corporation in which he owned the stock, and he transferred all the assets of our company into his. He then announced that *our* company was out of business, but *his* company was doing quite well, with great expectations for the future!

I brought a lawsuit to correct the situation, and both the trial and appeals courts held in my favor. They said that my partner's new corporation was in fact the property of our original corporation.

Unfortunately, this legal triumph turned out to be a classic Pyrrhic victory. In other words, even though I won, I lost. We still had equal representation on the board of directors, and all the officers of the company were his people. Because I had only a 50 percent interest, I couldn't marshal a majority to get his people out. He, in contrast, was in a position to take out the company profits in the form of salaries, profit sharing, bonuses, stock options, country club memberships, company cars, insurance policies, you name it.

So in this case, the fifty-fifty deal once again proved to be my undoing. Finally, I sold the company to my partner for less than it was actually worth just to escape all the headaches and hassles.

MISTAKE #2: THE PERILS OF CERTAIN PRODUCTS

Sometimes, my fatal mistakes have focused on the product the company put out. The most obvious kind of product blunder, of course, is to try to sell something nobody wants to buy. That often happens when an entrepreneur "falls in love" with an item instead of looking at it with a cold, hard eye, in light of the realities of the marketplace. Or your product may have a market, but you can't produce it economically enough to turn a decent profit.

My product problems, however, have often proven to be more subtle. One time, a fellow came to us with an idea for an exciting new machine designed to perform a rather esoteric function in certain manufacturing companies. Because it was extremely expensive to produce, I knew everything had to be just right before we took it out into the marketplace.

So I told the entrepreneur he should be especially thorough in field-testing it before any attempt was made to sell it to a customer. He seemed to agree, and I didn't pursue the matter any further. That was my fatal error. Moreover, I compounded the problem by entering into this venture on an equal-partner arrangement.

Soon after we'd signed the contract, my young partner insisted to my dismay that it wasn't necessary in this case to do the customary field-testing. I protested, "It's going to be a disaster!"

But he replied, "No, you don't have to worry! We know exactly what we are doing."

With the fifty-fifty arrangement, I couldn't put my foot down. I *knew* that we were heading down the road to total disaster. But

I suppose I was hoping against hope that I had missed something. Perhaps I was wrong and the other guy was right, I thought.

Also, being an impatient person, I didn't have much inclination to get involved in a standoff with this other fellow. I just lacked interest in the conflict.

So he forged ahead without testing the equipment thoroughly. He took it directly into various plants and had his people start assembling it. Before long, the magnitude of the mistake began to surface.

First of all, the technicians, who had handled the equipment only minimally in our warehouse, didn't have a clue about what they were doing in the assembly process. We asked them to take it apart and put it back together again at least ten times before shipping.

"There's no way this machine is not going to work!" they protested.

A reverse prophesy, confirmed by a coup de grâce: They hooked it up to the wrong kind of current and burned out all the mctors!

With some companies, this blunder might have presented some serious problems or setbacks which could still have been overcome. But for us, because of the high cost of the machinery (which ran into the tens of thousands of dollars) this mistake completely wrecked the company and its reputation.

This particular "mistake" is really several mistakes rolled into one. Certainly, the foulup began with the old blunder of the fifty-fifty deal. But the biggest problem, in my mind, was the product problem, which they might have been able to avoid if they had just had more experience, or listened to more experienced people.

MISTAKE #3: GOING PUBLIC

Although I list this point as a mistake, I want to emphasize that it's a mistake that's quite personal to me. Some entrepreneurs can achieve great success and remain very happy and satisfied with a public company. But not me!

After having run private companies for a number of years,

I began to watch other entrepreneurs who seemed able to do great things after they had "gone public"—or been listed on a stock exchange with shares which could be bought and sold by the general public. It all seemed so big-time and glamorous that I was sure I would thrive in that kind of environment. But I was wrong.

The public company was a conglomerate that owned steel mills, forging companies, electrical switching companies, lock companies, design companies and many others. I owned 51 percent of the stock, so I had complete control over the operation.

But as it turned out, the issue of control wasn't what bothered me. I didn't realize until I had begun to operate as a public corporation that I simply didn't like to do business this way.

For one thing, I just didn't want the responsibility of playing nursemaid to thousands of stockholders, regardless of how much extra money that might mean I could make. Also, I didn't want to go to analysts' meetings and various board functions. Nonproductive meetings absolutely drive me up a wall! Furthermore, government regulations and requirements proliferated at an alarming rate when we got into the public arena.

So after a short time, I decided that this way of doing business was not for me, and I sold my interest. I also resolved never again to go public—primarily because it just didn't fit my personality.

This was not a mistake that cost me any money. In fact, I *made* money in the process of going public. But what I did lose was an inner sense of well-being, a serenity which evaporated when I mounted the public stage.

Among the things that can really threaten your sense of personal peace when you're trying to run a public company are the politics and piratical tactics that sometimes flourish in the nation's public boardrooms. This is especially true if you're *not* the majority shareholder. The threat of mergers and takeovers from the outside is always present with public operations these days. Many of my friends have been heartbroken by getting thrown out of companies they started.

But just as often, subversion many come from within. The histories of the nation's corporations are rife with examples of what I call the "Brutus in the boardroom." In other words, you may think you've done an excellent job of picking a board that supports you to the hilt. You may also believe that these people are not only your business colleagues but also your friends. But if it comes to a big showdown, where control of the company and huge amounts of money are involved, your greatest buddy may very well vote against you.

Suppose, for example, you allow control of the company to slip away from you—so that, let's say, you have 40 or 45 percent of the ownership instead of 51 percent. In such a case, it might take only a few of these former "friends" to put you out on the street.

True, there are plenty of outstanding entrepreneurs who have made the transition from the private to the public arena. But I've also run into quite a few of them who wish they had never gone public.

Usually, you want to be listed on one of the stock exchanges in order to pull in a great deal more money. This is done through a public offering to the nation's shareholders through brokerage houses. But what you gain in that extra financing may very well be lost in privacy and peace of mind. In my view, the corporate jets and other fringe benefits aren't worth the extra headaches. My style is to stay smaller and continue to own all or most of an enterprise.

MISTAKE #4: FAILURE TO GET TOUGH IN NEGOTIATING THE BASIC CONTRACT

When you're drawing up a contract with a prospective business partner—and especially if you have only a minority or equal interest—it's important to include some clear-cut escape clauses or "right of entry" provisions. These will allow you to take over the business or sell it in case your business buddy doesn't live up to certain agreed-upon profit projections.

I failed to take these precautions in what I call my "Canadian caper," and believe me, I'll never make that error again.

Some young businessmen approached me with what looked like a surefire deal to buy a company in Canada. We agreed that I would put up 75 percent of the money and they would put up

25 percent. Also, they would personally guarantee any bank loans that were taken out.

But you never get to know people really well until you've done business with them for a while. In this case, the young men had at first seemed entirely competent. In fact, they *were* quite accomplished in many aspects of business. But what they didn't understand very well were some of the subtleties of international high finance. Unfortunately, the big issue in this company revolved around some of the most difficult financial issues imaginable. And my partners were soon out of their depth.

In brief, the issue centered on whether or not they could get financing from a Canadian bank. The bank had to be Canadian because of the exchange laws in that country. But it wasn't just a simple matter of walking in the door, presenting our business plan and endorsing the note. Rather, we also had to have the approval of the Canadian government. Moreover, the owners of the company wouldn't sell without Canadian approval. They were afraid that somehow, if the Canadian government balked, they might be stuck with the plant.

In other words, we ran into a "Catch-22" type of impasse: The Canadian government wouldn't give its approval without our owning the company; yet the bank wouldn't grant us a loan without government approval. The deal quickly became too big and complicated for my partners—who had assured me they already had the bank loan. To make matters worse, they became frightened and panicked because of the large amount of money involved.

The upshot was that the Canadian government's approval never came through; the entire sales negotiation ground to a halt. Soon, other interested buyers began to make headway in trying to buy the company out from under us.

As I sat on the sidelines, watching this scenario unfold, I was really frustrated. Several alternative methods of financing had come to my attention, but I couldn't move because my partners wouldn't agree to step aside. Finally, we did manage to put together a rather creative financing arrangement which would undoubtedly have worked. But then at the eleventh hour, the company was sold out from under us to a competing Canadian corporation. And the company is now making a million dollars a month!

I was furious at this outcome; but at the same time, I had to admit that the result was entirely my own fault. My mistake went back to the basic contractual arrangement that I had with my young partners.

I would have been willing to give them as much freedom as they required in the initial phases of the venture. But then, when they began to run into roadblocks, I should have been able to take over the negotiations and finalize the deal in my own way. They could have stayed in or dropped out, whichever they wanted. Such an arrangement would have been quite reasonable—especially since I put up 75 percent of the cash. But because they said they had already put the deal together, I didn't push for control under these circumstances—and that was my big mistake.

In retrospect, I can see that the wise thing would have been to include a clause in the basic contract that would have allowed us to move in under certain conditions of failure. So I took the lesson to heart: I resolved that in all future deals I would insist upon the right to take over within a certain time period if the partner failed to meet within reasonable limits certain projections or goals.

This the way most venture capitalists operate these days. These types of projects *have* to work, or the enormous amounts of time and money spent on them will be lost. So some means of salvaging a faltering venture have to be built into the basic contractual arrangement.

MISTAKE #5: THE BUREAUCRATIC BLUNDER

While traveling in Europe a few years ago, I noticed that there seemed to be a tremendous upsurge in building prefabricated houses and office space. In some cases, the structures were really beautiful. So I decided that if this product was doing so well in Europe, it should absolutely *explode* in the United States.

My reasoning? For one thing, the prices of prefab buildings

could be kept quite low in comparison with ordinary housing. Also, if the demand proved to be as great as I expected, the market for these structures could be phenomenal.

I was very bullish on this concept when I returned to the United States, and I immediately took steps to set up an enterprise which would build these prefabricated structures. Everything seemed to go very well—until I ran head on into the local real estate bureaucracy.

My main mistake was that I had looked at the idea with the eye of an entrepreneurial purist. To be sure, I had evaluated the product, the management requirements and the expected demand from the public. But I was thinking in a vacuum. I had forgotten all about the red tape that often accompanies building projects in the United States.

In the first place, I had overlooked the fact that I would have to get building permits every time I wanted to put a structure up. You often have to wait ages to get those permits; and that sort of delay can play havoc with production schedules. We found that we had huge inventories building up which we couldn't sell because the go-ahead hadn't come through from the government.

Also, there was some community resistance. Neighbors were afraid that prefabricated housing would lower the quality of housing in the neighborhood. This required other government meetings, approvals and permits.

Finally, there was a cultural problem. Americans, in general, don't like prefab housing. Thy prefer individual styling.

Before long, it became apparent to me that the business simply wasn't going to work. We couldn't possibly coordinate all the government requirements and red tape with a profitable sales schedule. So we quit and moved on to something else.

I don't want to suggest that it's not possible to make a good profit in this sort of real estate venture. There are plenty of entrepreneurs who get along quite well in this area. But they are the ones who do what I *didn't* do: They take the government requirements into consideration and ensure that red tape doesn't strangle their venture before it even gets started.

MISTAKE #6: GREED

A number of years ago, I thought I had stumbled onto the perfect entrepreneurial deal. But I let my desire to make a quick killing—in short, my greed—distort my judgment. As a result, I forgot some clear investment principles that I had always followed.

It happened in a foreign country, where a millionaire decided to build a $35 million club. At the time, it was one of the best luxury facilities of its type in the world. He built 200 rooms, two eighteen-hole golf courses and an incredible dining area that could have served a thousand-room hotel.

Also, I learned that an investment company, a high-flyer in the 1960s and early 1970s, had lent $5 million to the project. And they had promised more.

When I caught wind of what was happening, I immediately scouted the area and found a sizable tract of land next to his property which was for sale. I thought, "If I don't buy it, I'll be furious with myself forever! I'll probably blow a $5 million profit."

I was certain that this was the perfect real estate deal. It was virtually inevitable, I believed, that the land would soar in price.

But what I hadn't banked on was the millionaire's complete lack of management ability and judgment in putting together a resort project like this. Also, although he had built 200 suites, that wasn't enough to keep his revenues up in the profitable range. In fact, it wasn't even the size of a good motel!

The upshot was that within a year and a half of my purchase of the adjoining land, the luxury resort was broke—and the millionaire's financial backers were in trouble. There I was, stuck with an unproductive investment.

I still own it, and I've even tried to do a little development on it. But the growth has headed in other directions, and I, quite frankly, have been the loser.

In retrospect, I can see that I allowed my fantasies about the fast buck to cloud my judgment on foreign real estate investments. A desire to make a lot of money the easy way made me forget a key investment principle that I've always followed: I've made it a point to *never* invest for profit in foreign property. Some people may be able to get involved in foreign real estate transactions profitably. But not me.

Once I owned a hotel on an island. The idea was to run a luxury facility that would be the ultimate Fantasy Island vacation spot for Americans in the Caribbean. But it just didn't work. We ran into problems with the local laws and with establishing a resort in that island culture. Every time I've tried something like that in a foreign country, I've lost my shirt.

What this all comes down to, I suppose, is simply discipline. You possess particular personality characteristics which no one else has, and you should always rely heavily on them when you're trying to decide on an entrepreneurial venture. Some things will work for you, and some things won't. When you get to know your entrepreneurial strengths, be sure to formulate a personal strategy which fits you as an individual—and then *stick to it*. Don't let greed, whim or anything else cause you to try to function outside of your proper entrepreneurial character.

MISTAKE #7: A LACK OF FORESIGHT
ABOUT THE ECONOMY

Everybody, but *everybody*, makes this mistake. In fact, I'm not even sure that it should be called a mistake. Maybe it's just bad luck when you plan a particular entrepreneurial strategy and then find that it doesn't work simply because of outside economic factors.

I still own what I was sure would be one of the best pieces of property of all time. It's seventy-five acres of prime industrial property near one of the nation's great cities— and I've been holding it for twenty years without a buyer in sight!

The land has been developed and sold all around this particular tract. But for some reason, the real estate that I bought was just a dog. I always thought it was worth more than what we could get somebody to pay; but *nothing* is *ever* worth more than somebody will pay!

I'm one who believes there's always a reason for everything. When you say there's no reason for something, that's a cop-out.

That's why I'll always analyze and then analyze again in an effort to figure out what went wrong with a particular project. But I can honestly say this is one mistake that I just haven't figured out.

One point that some people have raised is that part of the property is near the end of an airplane runway. But it's not a big commercial airport—it's a military facility with relatively little activity. That shouldn't have bothered businesses which might have been concerned about high noise levels. In fact, various industrial plants have been built in the same area.

So I guess I'll just have to chalk this up to one of the quirks of the local economy, or some other such uncontrollable fluke. It's a mistake that I have to live with, but not one which I feel I could have corrected at the time. I simply had no way of knowing what would go wrong.

So, sometimes, things are going to go wrong which simply can't be anticipated. In fact, even as you examine them in retrospect, you may still never be able to figure out the source of the problem.

In the same way, you may not understand what's happening if the prospects for an investment do a quick turnaround. I may hold on to that property for another five or ten years, and then suddenly there may be an eruption of economic expansion in that area. In fact, I may find myself holding one of my greatest real estate investments! But you know as well as I do that such a result won't indicate I'm so smart. If I make a profit, it won't be because I anticipated this venture was going to be a winner decades down the road. Rather, I'll succeed because I was just plain lucky.

In fact, had I really been smart, I would have sold that property years ago for whatever I could get. The first loss is always the cheapest. So, don't allow yourself to get frustrated or discouraged if something unexpected and inexplicable happens in one of your early entrepreneurial outings. Things get off track for everybody at one time or another. When that happens, usually it's best to sell a losing or disappointing business for what you can get for it; stop worrying about any loss; and then move on to the next profitable opportunity. (If only I always followed my own advice!)

MISTAKE #8: FAILING TO KEEP
BOTH FEET ON THE GROUND

To some extent, all entrepreneurs live in a dreamworld. Their outrageous fantasies are what spur them on to great accomplishment.

Sometimes, however, a problem may develop when fantasy completely replaces the reality of the marketplace. I've run into a number of entrepreneurs who are absolutely convinced that they have a product which should command a certain price. Apparently unfamiliar with the fundamentals of price-testing, they stubbornly hold out for the highest price. The result: Many times they completely price themselves out of business.

Remember: A product is only worth what somebody is willing to pay for it. That's the reason that top marketing experts, such as those that deal in direct mail, will test several prices before they settle on the best one for their main marketing thrust. They want to be sure they sell at a price that will bring in the maximum profit.

An inexperienced entrepreneur, in contrast, might throw all his capital into selling the best-made backscratcher in the world for $30. There might in fact be a big market out there for backscratchers. But there's a big problem if most people are only willing to pay $19.95 for a backscratcher—and absolutely no one is willing to lay out $30. Too often, an inventor falls in love with his product and overprices it for the average consumer.

So the venture will fail because the entrepreneur insists on living in his dreamworld where his prices are not fixed by the marketplace. Yet it might have succeeded if he had tested a range of different prices before committing all his resources in the wrong direction.

This backscratching example may not be quite as farfetched as it sounds. My own little backscratching fallacy emerged in the form of a piece of property down in San Antonio. I had owned a condominium project with 220 apartments, and then I sold the entire place—with the exception of one unit I particularly liked. Later, however, I decided to sell the last one, and that was where I ran into some problems.

The project is located in a nice area, and I decided my remaining unit was worth $90,000 and not a penny less. That was my big mistake.

I waited one year, then two, and finally three. But no takers. So I got a bright idea. First, I put together some computer spread sheets on the apartment, just to see how much it was costing me each year. The annual cost, including taxes, refurbishing and maintenance, came to about $9,000.

Then, I began to do some more figuring: If I had sold that apartment for considerably less, say $75,000 to $80,000, I could have picked up about another $8,000 in interest on the money from the sale. In other words, as I waited for the perfect price, it was costing me at least $17,000 each year to keep that apartment.

After going through this cold, hard-nosed analysis, I was no longer so sure of myself. In fact, I decided immediately to put the apartment on the market for $80,000, and I was quite willing to sell it for $75,000, which is what someone was willing to pay. As you can see, even at a sale of $75,000 (a reduction of $15,000 on my "perfect price") I'd still be ahead of the $17,000 I was currently losing on that apartment each year at the $90,000 price.

The lesson? You simply can't get emotionally involved in your business ventures. You're out to make a profit, not to fall in love with a piece of property or a pet product. When it's not possible to achieve a profit, take your loss and run!

If you hope to succeed as an entrepreneur, it's absolutely essential that you learn to analyze your mistakes scientifically. The key is to learn what you've done wrong so that you can avoid the same errors in the future.

Yet most business people at one stage or another in their careers get into a rut. They rise to a certain level; but then they begin repeating a certain mistake or mistakes that they've been making all their lives.

Many salespeople do this. They'll ask the same wrong question or raise the same wrong issue over and over again. And that will kill the sale time after time.

You'll probably avoid many of the mistakes that I made, just because you're a different person. On the other hand, you're sure to make a number of mistakes that I never thought of. But just remember: Those obstacles on which you're stubbing your toe today can, with a little thought and foresight, become stepping stones to success tomorrow. If it's any encouragement, considering the number of businesses and properties I've owned in the past thirty years, the number of mistakes has been few and the losses minor—at least, in contrast to the winners.

Fourteen

Axioms for Entrepreneurs

"Wisdom, whose lessons have been represented as so hard to learn by those who never were at her school, only teaches us to extend a simple maxim universally known."

—Henry Fielding,
The History of Tom Jones

*L*et's take a step back and try to sum up the key points and principles on which many successful businesses may be built. There are, indeed, certain universal rules of the marketplace which don't go in and out of style. They are absolutes.

Here, then, are a few of my "Axioms for Entrepreneurs":

Ignorance is bliss. If an entrepreneur knew all the pitfalls he might stumble upon, he'd never get started.

A successful business venture requires a three- to five-year commitment. Although we always believe success will come tomorrow, that never happens. Great achievement always takes a little longer than we expect.

Down deep, everybody wants to run his own business. The reason: If you work for someone else, you'll always be restrained. Yet every human being alive wants to be free.

Reward should be based on merit—a point to remember when you're setting salary and bonuses.

Freedom of choice is a fundamental right. So the more freedom you can give your competent employees in management decision making, the happier and more effective they will be.

Every successful entrepreneur must have a good lawyer and a good accountant—but a good lawyer is the hardest to find.

Every business needs both youth and gray hair. Such skills as production and financial management come only with experience.

To succeed, an entrepreneur needs enough money, enough guts and plenty of support from a spouse.

Every successful business venture is based on a well-planned and executed concept of missions, goals, implementation and follow-through.

The most effective style of management is based on consensus decision making for 80–90 percent of company decisions. You may have to be the "captain" on 10–20 percent of decisions.

Assume that every new venture will cost twice what you expect it to cost.

The most successful business people love business first, family second and sports and everything else third.

Always try to own at least 51 percent of every new venture you start—at least, that's my personal view, given my type of personality and experience.

If you can't get 51 percent, negotiate a clause in the contract which will allow you to take over the company if the partners fail to meet certain goals and projections. (Of course, this solution assumes you're experienced enough to do a better job yourself or to hire managers who can do better. Otherwise, the contract clause should just allow you to sell the business to outsiders.)

Every great enterprise arises in response to a deep public need.

Every successful business person has identified and learned to harness his deepest drives and motives.

Evaluate all prospective partners, employees and business colleagues on the basis of their experience, personality, integrity, status, intelligence and appearance.

Good judgment is based 80 percent on knowledge and experience and 20 percent on intuition (of which 10 percent is subconscious knowledge and experience).

When you're young and have nothing to lose, you'll have to give your guarantee to loans for your entrepreneurial ventures. When you get older and stand to lose the wealth you've amassed, *never* put your personal guarantee on a loan or other obligation. At this stage of life, you should never be in a position to lose more than you can afford to lose.

Spread your loan obligations around among several banks so that one can't put you out of business.

Keep an idea book with you at all times.

The best business ideas are related to human needs.

Be scientific in monitoring business expenses.

Venture capitalists must be convinced that (1) your product is superior, (2) your management skills are outstanding, and (3) all partners in a project will be reliable.

Prepare well in advance to cross the half-million to million-dollar "border" that separates your business from the big time.

The first million is always harder to make than the second.

Your product cost must never exceed 50 to 60 percent of your sales price. (It's helpful to have a breakdown of typical industry costs, for the sake of comparison.)

Under some circumstances, practically every venture capital company will want some control over your enterprise—and that may be good for business!

The best businesses are built on good service, quality, ingenuity and efficiency.

Competent lower-level managers can often do more for entrepreneurs than chief executive officers.

An inefficient manager always wants more people on staff than an efficient manager.

Brace yourself psychologically for legal problems.

Analyze every mistake.

Think twice before you go public with your corporation—unless you want to "bail out" with the high profits that may accompany a public offering.

Protect your outside production system from pirates by (1) using more than one subcontractor, and (2) retaining control over the ultimate assembly of the product. A key here is the employment of unrelated subcontractors to execute the assembly process.

Most failures result from poor management, a poor product or a bad economy.

Eat well and exercise regularly.

Fifteen

The Fastest Gun in the West

---

*"What's good for America is good for you.
You are America."*

—*Warren Avis*

At some level, everybody wants to be the best. There's something in each of us that says, "I'd really like to be the *top* person in this field . . . on this project . . . with this idea."

Too often, though, we allow that inherent urge to win to be pushed aside or submerged. A failure, a mediocre performance or a series of distractions may make us willing to settle for less than the best. Often, coming in first, despite the odds of life, coincides with two personal qualities: (1) the ability to get a broad, sweeping perspective on difficult circumstances and setbacks; and (2) a willingness to dedicate oneself totally to achieving certain goals, no matter what the obstacles and risks may be.

I really don't think I'm too different from most entrepreneurs in this regard. When I first began to express my entrepreneurial impulses at a very young age, buying and selling one bicycle at a time, I certainly wanted to be the best at what I was doing. Also, I think I had a special knack for business. For a while, I succeeded rather well and even branched out into buying and selling used cars, also one at a time. As a result, I made a good bit of money by the time I was a teenager.

But then the Great Depression hit, and I was out of business just like everybody else. I had some bikes on hand, but nobody was buying, and at first I really didn't have a clue about what was going on. I even wondered if I had lost my touch as a salesman. In short, I failed to realize the problem wasn't with me, but rather with the economy at large.

That scenario is replayed over and over again in the experience of entrepreneurs, and it's easy to get discouraged. In my case, though, I decided to try again, even though I had lost my shirt. So at age seventeen, I set up a bicycle rental business through a large store in a local resort area and they rented the bikes for me. I even talked a big distributor into selling me bicycles on credit. With an improving economy, I managed to make some good money on this second business outing.

Of course, I didn't understand why the general economic conditions had destroyed my first venture. But later, as I got older and more experienced, I began to see how all my specialized business interests were dependent to one degree or another on the ups and downs of a larger economy. This increased understanding enabled me to plan my more mature business expansions and plan for the inevitable setbacks.

We all start off in a fairly similar position. The main difference between a champion in any field and an also-ran is commitment and dedication. There's no such thing as being number one in any endeavor without a superior level of devotion to the task at hand and to the achievement of that final, big goal far out into the future.

So when you're starting out with a new venture, resolve that you're going to put in plenty of time—a minimum of ten to twelve hours a day—just to learn the ropes and get your venture off the ground. It takes that kind of nose-to-the-grindstone mentality to get to first base in today's marketplace.

Even with this kind of work, you may very well fall flat on your face with your first effort, your second and even your third. But eventually, if you're consistently trying to learn and apply proven business principles, your efforts will begin to bear fruit. That *has* to happen! It's a principle built into the very fabric of the universe! If you have a modicum of intelligence, if you keep learning from your mistakes, and if you continue to follow a sound business game plan—then you *must* succeed!

I can point to countless entrepreneurs who have had the discipline to "stay with it" through thick and thin. Then, when they look back after, say, ten years' hard, well-planned effort, they see that they're doing much better than they were when they started out.

When you think about it, it's inevitable that this progress and improvement would take place. After ten years, you've got more experience; you've got more knowledge; and probably your basic intuitions and instincts are more finely honed than they were when you were younger and less wise in the ways of the business world.

Now, you're more than a lonely gunslinger: You've been through some battles and you've suffered some wounds; but you've survived in high style. Confidence has replaced uncertainty. You have taken the chance to be first, and constantly kept in mind the most basic rule of business success: "There is always room at the top!"

Appendix

One of the best ways we've discovered to evaluate various costs and expenses in a specific company is to study a variety of similar companies in the same industry and then to formulate a model expense analysis sheet. Such a sheet is helpful to venture capitalists as they evaluate whether to put their money into a given company. Specifically, a venture capitalist can compare the model expense sheet with the business plan from an individual company to see if the company's proposed expenses are in line with reality.

Also, a model expense analysis sheet can be quite helpful in keeping an entrepreneur or business person on track when he or she is starting up a new company or managing an older one. It's especially useful in signaling whether expenses have been omitted or underestimated.

To understand what I'm talking about, take a look at the model expense analysis sheet below for a manufacturing company in the metals industry. The far left-hand column contains the breakdown of certain expenses by name. The far right-hand column reflects the percentage of gross sales for each expense item in a typical, reasonably successful company in the industry. Finally, the middle column contains the ideal percentages the *most* successful companies should shoot for.

TYPE OF EXPENSE (Gross sales = 100%)	OPTIMUM % OF GROSS SALES FOR EACH EXPENSE	TYPICAL INDUSTRY % OF GROSS SALES FOR EACH EXPENSE
Sales Tax	4.00	4.00
Returns & Allowances	.20	.25
Adjusted Gross Sales	95.80	95.75
Sales Expenses		
Discounts	2.00	2.00
Commission	5.00	5.00
Warranty Expense	1.00	2.00
Bad Debt Expense	.50	1.00
Royalty Expense	—	—
Salaries—Sales	4.00	4.25
Salaries—Marketing	1.00	1.50
Salaries—Advertising	—	—
Fringe Benefits		
FICA	.36	.39
Unemployment Insurance	.18	.19
Workers' Compensation	.09	.10
Insurance	.30	.90
Pension	.30	.50
Bonuses	2.00	1.00
Promotional Expense	1.00	1.00
Travel	3.00	2.75
Entertainment	.40	.50
Advertising	4.00	3.00
Miscellaneous	.40	.50
Total Sales Expenses	25.03	25.58
Cost of Goods Sold		
Material	20.00	19.00
Labor	8.00	9.00
Direct Manufacturing Costs	2.00	2.20
Total Cost of Goods Sold	30.00	30.20
Operating Expenses		
Rent	2.00	1.75
Rental Equipment	.20	—

TYPE OF EXPENSE (Gross sales = 100%)	OPTIMUM % OF GROSS SALES FOR EACH EXPENSE	TYPICAL INDUSTRY % OF GROSS SALES FOR EACH EXPENSE
Maintenance & Repair	.60	.75
Telephone	.40	.35
Gas	.75	.75
Electricity	1.25	1.40
Water & Sewer	.15	.20
Supplies	.20	.15
Freight In	.20	.20
Freight Out	1.60	1.70
Auto Expense	.60	.70
Depreciation	1.00	1.00
Outside Services	.36	.30
Salaries	1.20	1.50
Fringe Benefits		
FICA	.16	.20
Unemployment Compensation	.10	.10
Workers' Compensation	.10	.10
Insurance	.24	.26
Packaging Supplies	.20	.40
Miscellaneous	.40	.60
Total Operating Expenses	10.71	12.41
General & Administrative Expenses		
Interest	2.00	2.50
Rent	—	.80
Telephone	.40	.30
Gas	.20	.21
Electricity	.20	.18
Water & Sewer	.10	.10
Salaries	6.00	5.00
Fringe Benefits		
FICA	.40	.40
Unemployment Compensation	.20	.20
Worker's Compensation	.10	.08
Insurance	.24	.30
Travel	.50	.50
Entertainment	.50	.40
Postage	.24	.20
State Income Tax	.80	.50
Depreciation	.20	.20

TYPE OF EXPENSE (Gross sales = 100%)	OPTIMUM % OF GROSS SALES FOR EACH EXPENSE	TYPICAL INDUSTRY % OF GROSS SALES FOR EACH EXPENSE
Amortization	—	1.00
Licenses & Fees	—	—
Dues & Subscriptions	.06	.08
Professional Fees	.50	.80
Bank Services Charge	—	—
Donations	—	—
Supplies	.20	.22
Auto Expenses	.60	.50
Insurance	.40	.65
Bonuses	1.20	—
Miscellaneous	.20	.40
Total General & Administrative Expenses	15.14	15.52
Net Income Before Federal Income Tax	19.92	12.04

A number of these expense items may catch the eye of a banker or venture capitalist—and influence your ability to get financing for your business. To give you some idea of possible red flags that may alienate a money source, here are a few "business plan blips," or major flaws and omissions.

Blip #1: The proposed product manufacturing costs are more than 50 to 60 percent of the sales price.

One entrepreneur sent a business plan which projected a couple of hundred thousand dollars of sales per year. But it was clear from the way the numbers were put together that the management had fallen far short in trying to reach previous goals in earlier years. In fact, they had expected to be at around a million dollars in sales at the time they contacted us, but at that point they had only reached small sales.

That might not have been so bad if only the relationship between the sales price of the product and the cost of producing the product hadn't been completely out of whack. The basic rule is that the manufacturing cost of the product can't exceed 50 to

60 percent of the sales price. If it does, you're on a fast track to disaster. (The term "product cost" includes the cost of materials, labor and manufacturing overhead.)

The company was in clear violation of this rule, even in the future projections of sales which they provided. Specifically, they had projected that in the next year, their total product cost would be $700,000 and the price at which they planned to sell the item would be one million. In other words, the product was going to cost about 70 percent of the projected sales price. They were broke before they started! Their high administrative and sales costs and overhead, which typically would run 30–40 percent of sales, left no room for profit.

The reason these percentage calculations are so important is that an entrepreneur will be lucky to make a 15 percent profit on his or her total sales after the operation really begins to hum. A successful manufacturing company will often make between 10 percent and 20 percent profit before taxes. So if the cost of the product is too high, you're automatically cutting back on your profit potential and may be setting yourself up for a loss. Clearly, just a small variation of 5–10 percent in what it costs to put out a product can mean the difference between success or failure.

In the manufacturing business we've been considering, the high product cost could have been an absolute disaster. There would have been no chance of a profit.

As you might expect, different businesses will require a different approach to these percentages. Generally speaking, it's best to set 60 percent as the absolute upper limit for what a product should cost in relation to the sales price. But when you're evaluating other types of companies—especially in the high-demand high-tech area, with computers and other sophisticated electronic products—you expect the product cost to be a much lower percentage of the sales price. Because a good high-tech product must get a big markup to penetrate a market, use 25–35 percent as a rule of thumb for these companies.

If such a favorable cost-price percentage can be combined with good management and a product with market potential, the chances are you're dealing with a winner.

So when you're drawing up a business plan, be sure you keep

a close watch on the percentage relationship between product cost and wholesale price. If you don't, you will probably fail.

Blip #2: A failure to include bad debts in your business plan.

Bad debts may run roughly around 1–2 percent of your gross sales. This may not seem like a great deal, but remember: These percentages are cutting directly into your future profit! So include a bad debt entry in your business plan. Almost no one ever does, yet that 1–2 percent can have a major impact on your profits.

In other words, the inclusion of a bad debt item shows that an entrepreneur has a completely realistic approach to his business prospects. Also he's probably a seasoned management expert, with some hands-on experience in the past with bad debts—or he's been advised by such an expert.

Finally, a bad debt entry says: "This guy pays attention and understands the importance of details—and detail can mean the difference between profit and loss in a new venture."

Blip #3: A failure to include a certain percentage for research and development expenses for a company that's expected to be on the "cutting edge" of an industry.

It's quite common for businesses that are involved with high-tech products or other new inventions to use 5 percent or even more of their gross sales income on research and development. They just can't stay up with the market unless they include this expense.

If this is the type of company you plan to be involved with, you should include this expense if you hope to look like you know what you're doing. In a very new company, you should put 5 percent or more into research and development—because that's what this budget item will begin to cost very soon, when you get just a little larger.

You may actually put a relatively small amount of money into R & D at first because *you personally* may be doing the research and you probably won't be charging the company for your time. Later, though, you'll hire someone to do the R & D, and it's important to anticipate that expense.

For example, in one high-tech company, we have about 0.5 percent of our gross sales income designated for research and development, even though we don't spend that much. It's important when you're drawing up a business plan for an innovation-oriented company, that *some* amount be designated for this purpose.

Blip #4: You should include a cost for sales in your business plan—even if you don't have a sales force.

This may seem like nonsense. In some entrepreneurial ventures, the company may plan to make some equipment or product for another specific company, with the understanding that this other company will buy all your products. In other words, the very reason you're setting up your company is to meet some special need of another organization.

So you may say, "I'm selling all I produce to a Fortune 500 Company, so I don't have any sales cost." But that's a mistake.

You see, *somebody* has to stay in touch with "Mister Big" or whoever your single buyer may be, to cultivate intercompany relationships. Also, it's necessary for someone to gather such information as how many of your products are needed; when they need to be delivered; and whether your company needs to consider making certain improvements in the product.

This means that you'll need to hire a manufacturer's representative or in-house salespeople. That will cost you probably between 3 percent and 5 percent of your gross sales. This item becomes quite important as you grow and attempt to forecast precise expenditures.

Of course, you, the founder and president of the company, may say, "Well *I'll* just make all those calls myself."

You may indeed be able to handle that part of the business yourself at first. But try adding up your out-of-pocket expenses, the value of your time and other such factors. You'll most likely find that the cost for you to perform this sales-related function will still come to between 3 percent and 5 percent of your gross sales. And when your business gets larger, you simply won't have time to make all the calls, and you'll *have* to hire a manufacturer's representative or in-house sales personnel.

These blips, as I've called them, are just a few of the items and omissions that may catch the eye of a seasoned venture capitalist. And they can put you in a favorable or unfavorable light, depending upon how you've handled them.

Of course, your industry will present you with certain norms of cost, and it's important to know what those are. As you grow, you can expect your costs to change like those of other similar companies. The main thing to remember is that you need to think your business idea through in minute detail. That definitely means doing more than slapping together a short business plan during an hour or so one evening. If you try that, you certainly won't have much chance of getting support from an experienced venture capitalist.

Index